Openings
A Meditation on History, Method, and Sumas Lake

British Columbia's Sumas Lake was drained in the 1920s to create farmlands in the Fraser Valley. This lake is the subject of Laura Cameron's *Openings*, a multifaceted exploration of the complex relationship between place and history. On one level it is a history of a lake and its "reclamation" as seen from the perspectives of various groups – Native people, bureaucrats, families, farmers. On another it is an innovative meditation on the historian's craft, locating the past not only in the fluid process of making oral history and the creative transformation of archival documents but also in the bonds people forge between stories and the places around them.

The "Opening" chapter reflects on the connection between historical and technological frontiers. "Listening for Pleasure" discusses oral histories as they relate to the negotiated and contested space of Sumas Lake. "Margins and Mosquitoes" recovers archival records from Victoria to Ottawa to explore flood-lake involvements federally, provincially, and locally. "Memory Device" moves into the archive of land and waterscapes, looking for connections between place and history, mindful of both Native oral tradition and written accounts of the lake. The concluding chapter, "One More Byte," written from the perspective of a mosquito, attempts to distance this project from the work of modernization while assessing the value of interactive history.

An independent but complementary hypermedia essay "Disappearing a Lake" is located on the World Wide Web at http://www.mcgill.ca/mqupress/opening/welcome.html.

LAURA CAMERON is a doctoral candidate in historical geography, Cambridge University.

Openings

A Meditation on
History, Method, and Sumas Lake

LAURA CAMERON

The University of British Columbia
Academic Women's Association

McGill-Queen's University Press
Montreal & Kingston · London · Buffalo

Printed in Canada on acid-free paper

This book has been published with the help of a grant from the Humanities and
Social Sciences Federation of Canada, using funds provided by the
Social Sciences and Humanities Research Council of Canada.

McGill-Queen's University Press acknowledges the support received for its
publishing program from the Canada Council's Block Grants program.

Canadian Cataloguing in Publication Data

Cameron, Laura, 1966–
Openings: a meditation on history, method, and Sumas Lake
Co-published by the University of British Columbia
Academic Women's Association.
Includes bibliographical references and index.
ISBN 0-7735-1666-2
1. Sumas Lake (B.C.) – Historical geography. 2. Historical geography – Case studies.
I. UBC Academic Women's Association.
FC3845.S92C34 1997   911′.71133   C97-900781-X
F1089.S92C34 1997

Published in cooperation with the University of British Columbia
Academic Women's Association

Consulting Editor
Dianne Newell

Editorial Board, UBC Academic Women's Association
Dianne Newell, Department of History and Faculty of Graduate Studies, General Editor
Alison Buchan, Department of Physiology
Diana Lary, Department of History

Contents

Maps / vi

Illustrations / vii

Foreword by Dianne Newell / ix

Preface / xv

Opening / 3

Listening for Pleasure / 16

Margins and Mosquitoes / 41

Memory Device / 76

One More Byte / 92

Notes / 97

Bibliography / 113

Index / 129

Maps

1 International Boundary Commission map, 1869 / 45

2 Hydrographic Survey map, 1912 / 47

3 "A Rough Diagram ... of Reserves Laid Off for Government Purposes,"
May 1864 / 52

4 Captain Jemmett's plan of Sumas Indian reserves,
New Westminster District, 1881–82 / 58

5 Lower Fraser Valley, showing main floodwater breeding areas at
21-foot river level, 1921 / 71

6 Key map of Sumas Reclamation Area, October 1919 / 73

Illustrations

Sumas lake bottom. View of Vedder Canal and Sumas Mountain / 4

Cousins swimming in Sumas Lake, *ca* 1897 / 17

Crew of the *Argo* on Sumas Lake *ca* 1897 / 17

Sumas Lake, 1913 / 20

The McConnell sisters at Bellrose, July 1920 / 20

Picnic at Sumas Lake, 1901 / 22

Skating party at Sumas Lake, 1905 / 25

Edward Kelly at Sumas, 1912 / 28

Sunday school picnic at Bellrose Station, *ca* 1918 / 28

Sumas Lake in flood, looking towards Lakeshore Ridge, *ca* 1912 / 30

Chief Ned, greeting visitors to the smokehouse, Kilgard, *ca* 1915 / 32

Beaver 2 tied up at Fook's Barn, Sumas Lake, *ca* 1905 / 35

Picnic on the shore of Sumas Lake, *ca* 1897 / 35

Canoeing in the dugout at high-water time, Sumas Lake, *ca* 1919 / 37

"B.C. Indian Leader Slams Germans, Greenpeace" / 39

Barbara Beldam and Muriel McPhail on the way to the Chilliwack
River lodge, 1921 / 42

Telegram from Lawrence Vankoughnet to Gilbert Sproat, 3 April 1879 / 56

Sharp-shinned hawk, Sumas, 1905 / 62

Part of the Brooks bird collection, *ca* 1930 / 64

Stó:lō fishermen with Fraser River catch, date unknown / 65

Sumas Lake, seen from the B.C. Electric substation on Vedder Mountain, *ca* 1916 / 75

Sumas Prairie, also from the substation, 1926 / 75

Stop of interest, Trans-Canada Highway / 77

Mr G at home, looking towards Sumas Prairie / 79

Painting of Sumas Lake by Mr G / 79

Louie Alexander painting beside Sumas Lake / 80

Painting of Sumas Lake by Louie Alexander / 80

McGregor Ridge / 90

Lakemount Marsh, a remaining part of Sumas Lake currently operated
by a private hunting club / 90

Autograph of Clytie (Bowman) Greeno in Ida (Bowman) Campbell's
autograph book / 95

Foreword

Laura Cameron's *Openings: A Meditation on History, Method, and Sumas Lake* is in the forefront of contemporary historical scholarship. In *Openings* Cameron experiments with connections between objects, such as computers, mosquitoes, and landscape – all powerful memory devices – and stories and storytellers. "Stories help orient us with respect to our lives and, in no small measure, with respect to the places in which we live," she writes. "Our storytellers invest places with meaning, and, reflexively, these places orient the stories they tell" (p. 78). Cameron's place is Sumas Lake, British Columbia. ("Sumas," which comes from the Stó:lō language of Halq'eméylem, can be translated as "big opening.") Drained in the 1920s in the spirit of progress through technology, Sumas became the intensely managed floodplain that it is today. Cameron's research was undertaken as part of her graduate work in the Department of History at the University of British Columbia.

The Academic Women's Association at the University of British Columbia promotes exciting new fields of women's scholarly inquiry by encouraging the publication of research results. *Openings* is the latest in the AWA's book series.

The first volume in the series, a work of history by Lee Stewart, *"It's Up To You": Women at UBC in the Early Years* (Vancouver: UBC Press, 1990), was intended as the

AWA's contribution to the university's seventy-fifth anniversary celebrations. Stewart examines the experience and strategies of female advocates, educators, and students against the background of the social and cultural conditions prior to the revolutionary decade of the 1960s.\

The second volume, *Women, Work, and Coping: A Multidisciplinary Approach to Workplace Stress* (McGill-Queen's University Press, 1993), takes as its focus employed women and investigates the special issue of coping with workplace stress today. It is a collection of original scholarly essays commissioned and edited by Bonita Long and Sharon Kahn, both of whom are professors in the Department of Counselling Psychology, Faculty of Education, University of British Columbia, and have been researching and writing on the subject since the early 1980s. The contribution by Allison Tom, "Women's Lives Complete: Methodological Concerns," received the Canadian Research Institute for the Advancement of Women's annual Marion Porter Prize for the most significant feminist research article.

Volume three of the series, which McGill-Queen's University Press also published this year, is Nancy Roberts's *Schools of Sympathy: Gender and Identification through the Novel*, a study of the role that reading novels can play in the formation of gender positioning. Roberts undertook the research for her doctoral thesis in English at the University of British Columbia, for which she won the AWA's A. Jean Elder dissertation prize. Nancy Roberts is a member of the faculty of Langara College in Vancouver.

On behalf of the AWA I wish to thank my colleagues on the editorial board, Alison Buchan and Diana Lary, and the current AWA chair, Susan Kennedy, director of the Occupational Hygiene Program of the Faculty of Graduate Studies. Philip Cercone, director and executive editor of McGill-Queen's University Press, has once again offered much-needed support at a critical stage of the project. A special thanks to others at the press, Aurèle Parisien, Joan McGilvray, and Gavin Twedily, who have responded to the imaginative qualities of this project with enthusiasm and skill. The manuscript won a much-appreciated grant-in-aid of publication from the Social Sciences Federation of Canada, using funds provided by the Social Sciences and Humanities Research Council of Canada. Finally, I wish to acknowledge the backing of the president of UBC, David Strangway, and the vice-president and provost, Daniel

R. Birch. Several years ago Dr Strangway authorized a generous grant from the University Development Fund to support the AWA book series and more recently authorized additional funding to help with the special production needs of this book project.

Dianne Newell
General Editor
AWA Series

Preface

Openings is a revised version of my MA thesis, "Openings to a Lake: Historical Approaches to Sumas Lake, British Columbia," which was completed in the Department of History, University of British Columbia, in 1994. The project began in 1993 with a hypermedia essay entitled "Disappearing a Lake: A Meditation on Method and Mosquitoes," which included many of the images, texts, and recordings that I had encountered during the research process. Lugging my (sometimes) trusty PowerBook 100 from one patient reader, listener, or writer to another, I gathered encouragement and critique for making the bound thesis that eventually followed. So began a productive though rather awkward relationship between my hypermedia and my printed text, which despite changing attitudes and changing software and hardware, remains uneasy. The forms are entangled: thus, I encourage those who have access to the World Wide Web to visit the McGill-Queen's website, http://mcgill.ca/mqupress/homepa.html, and browse through the web version of the earlier Hyper-Card essay.

Without the unfailing support of my research supervisor Dianne Newell and without Peter Ward's keen interest in new approaches to Canadian history in his graduate seminar, the lake project would have dried up before it got started. Matt Rogalsky's electronic creativity sustained the project throughout. I would like to thank the UBC Academic Women's Association, which selected my manuscript for its publication series, and Dianne Newell and the editorial committee for mentoring it through the thesis-to-book process and raising funds to subsidize the project.

Sandra Dyck, Leonard Kuffert, Albert "Sonny" McHalsie, Susan Neylan, Allan Smith, Neil Smith, and Peter Ward were the first to try out the HyperCard stack, and their insights provoked much rethinking in the early stages of the research process. La Verne Adams, Heather Cameron, Larry Commodore, Robert Galois, Don Goodes, R. Cole Harris, Doug Hudson, Anne Mohs, Gordon Mohs, Doug Nicol, Steve Straker, Barry Leach, Robert McDonald, and Bob Smith provided critical suggestions. For feedback and/or encouragement on the manuscript or portions of it, I extend my thanks to W.M. Adams, Alan R.H. Baker, Keith Carlson, Julie Cruikshank, Sandra Dyck, Gerald Hartnett, Philip Howell, Patsy Kotsopoulos, Donna Kwon, Linda McDowell, Neil Monckton, Muriel Morris, Dianne Newell, Arthur Ray, Janice Silver, Doug Steinson, Brian Thom, Frank Tough, and Peter Ward. The anonymous readers for UBC Press and McGill-Queen's University Press and the Aid to Scholarly Publications Program provided many helpful comments. A version of chapter 1 that appeared as "Listening for Pleasure" in *Native Studies Review* 11, no. 1, also benefited from the critique it received. At McGill-Queen's University Press, the project was very fortunate in meeting up with the skills of editor Aurèle Parisien, coordinating editor Joan McGilvray, editor Carlotta Lemieux, and the technical support of Gavin Twedily. Mike Young of the Drawing Office, Department of Geography, Cambridge, gave his cartographic expertise and good humour.

Many other individuals and organizations have contributed to *Openings* by putting me in touch with critical readings and research material, and to them I am deeply grateful. The private photograph and manuscript collections of Neil Smith, a farmer and historian in Sumas, provided many afternoons of absorbing study. Special mention must go to Jenny Anderson, Ethel Austin, Eleanor Blatchford, Jim Bowman, George Brandak, British Columbia Archives and Record Services, J.B. Cameron, Jody Cameron, William Chase, the Chilliwack Museum and Historical Society, the City of Vancouver Archives, the Coqualeetza Archives, Edward Dahl, Ron Denman, John Dornan, Edna Douglas, James Duncan, George Ferguson, Myrtle Ferguson, Paul Ferguson, Kris Foulds, Allan Furnell, Allan Guinet, Gerry Kearns, Delavina Kelly, Edward Kelly, Hugh Kelly, Naydeen Kelly, Denis Knopf, Anne Knowlan, Verna Leon, Betty McConnell, Bruce MacFayden, the Matsqui-Sumas-Abbotsford Museum Society, David

Mattison, Lloyd Michaud, Lynne Morgan, Rachel Munroe, the National Archives of Canada, Lester Ned, Maryanne Pope, Rudy Rogalsky, Sharon Rogalsky, Betty Rogers, Bill Russell, Janice Silver, Ray Silver Sr, Deb Stewart, Kelly Stewart, Stó:lō Nation Canada, Sumas Band, UBC Special Collections, the Vancouver Public Library, Birch Van Horne, Frances Woodward, and Frank Wright.

I also extend many thanks to my fellow students and friends Jennifer Baum, Judith Bronstein, David Clemis, Elizabeth Dougherty, Margaret Gallagher, Vanessa Geary, Mirjana Lausevic, Robert McGeachy, Wayne Melvin, Van Nguyen-Marshall, Hannah Moore, Arlene Oak, Lara Perry, Joanne Poon, Ben Redekop, Daryl Rose, Marla Rurka, Anne Russell and Sandy Tait for comfort and conversation. For inspiration, I am indebted to the generosity and creativity of the Rogalsky and Cameron families in all their extended variations. This book is dedicated to my partner Matt and to my great-aunt the British Columbian local historian Margaret Lang Hastings.

A note on language: The problematic terms "Euro-Canadian" and "white" describe myself and other people of European descent. I use the terms "Aboriginal," "Native," and "First Nations" interchangeably to refer to British Columbia's original inhabitants. The Stó:lō about whom I write are Aboriginal people living in the Lower Fraser drainage basin of southwestern British Columbia. Following ordinary legal usage in Canada, I use the term "Indian" to refer to people (and entities such as Indian reserves) so defined in the Indian Act. I also use the names that appear in the historical record, and in direct quotations I have retained the terms that were used.

25 November 1996

Openings

Opening

OPENING, n. 1. an act or instance of making or becoming open. 2. an unobstructed or unoccupied space or place. 3. a hole or void in solid matter. 4. the act of beginning: start. 5. the first part or initial stage of anything. 6. an employment vacancy. 7. an opportunity; chance. 8. a. the formal or official beginning of an activity, event, presentation, etc. b. a celebration marking this. 9. the statement of the case made by legal counsel to the court or jury before presenting evidence. 10. a mode of beginning a game: *chess openings.*[1]

The word "opening" has many possible meanings. In certain contexts, many levels of meaning may exist simultaneously. One such context is the moment a person sits down at a computer to begin to write a history about a place in the West, the North American West. Here is an opportunity to open a new document electronically, to open the mind creatively, to make a first move in the academic game, and to start to make a case. Diving into the void – the future of the past – with anticipatory celebration, the historian surfaces sometime around June 1808. Gasping and sputtering for air, lo and behold, trembling hands grasp a folder of written documents. The sea parts, the folder opens to reveal the journal of Simon Fraser, the European who was searching for liquid openings to the Pacific via Stó:lō, the river that would soon carry his name. The opening to new frontiers! "To boldly go …"

Sumas lake bottom. View of Vedder Canal from Vedder Mountain, looking north towards
Sumas Mountain. The Fraser River runs behind Sumas Mountain
(photo by L. Cameron, January 1994)

The project within, from beginning to open-end, is a brief engagement with a lake – an opening between water and history, the interplay linking the stuff of nature and its historical representation within culture. The entry point is specific, local, and currently nonexistent: a southwestern British Columbian lake whose name, Sumas, translates as "big opening."[2] Sumas Lake, a large, sometimes shallow lake in the Lower Fraser Valley of British Columbia, was drained in the 1920s, and a complex and costly drainage system was installed to pump water from the valuable[3] agricultural and residential lands. Engineers report that if this artificial draining ceased, most of the 22,000 acres of the lake bottom would again be covered with water.[4] To imagine such a future is to recall the area's past, which was – I am reminded by the Chilliwack man who developed my Sumas Lake Bottom photographs in 1994 – "a different country."[5]

Openings can be treacherous. In the planning stages, my introduction explored roots in European theory, crossed to North American historiography, went westering, and tied up with an attempt to legitimize a pioneering hypertextual approach to history. I belatedly realized that this direction and attitude had placed me firmly inside Simon Fraser's canoe. Canoeing downstream on the chronological paper trail, we pass a place where "the river expands into a lake."[6] No matter how loath we are to share in Simon Fraser's colonial venture, the desire to find or create openings may lead us to make and honour the same strokes as the white explorers and settlers who went westering in the territory of the Stó:lō not so long ago. We reify the irreverent and ignorant claim that what makes British Columbian history interesting – ideas, colourful characters, change – came from elsewhere. The time of the river and the traditions of its people are reduced, in the phrase of the economic historian Harold Adams Innis, to an "absolute nullity."[7] As the "big opening" of Sumas Lake is represented with new theory or computer technology, it must also be approached with new respect.

Self-examination is thus in order. A focus on objects – a lake and a computer – may reflect a desire to connect with physical "things" in order to mitigate increasing disorientation in one of the most rapidly changing landscapes of Canada. Putting a lake (typically seen as a part of nature) in the same category as a computer (a supposed item of culture) might appear somewhat mixed up. But both really are mixtures of nature and culture. As Bruno Latour, a European scholar who often teaches in the

North American West, tells us, "the very notion of culture is an artifact created by bracketing Nature off."[8] People interact with a lake and a computer, shaping them with real matter, discourse, and collective action.[9] Simultaneously, these things alter people, the real world, language, and politics.

I must admit that in terms of reorienting one's perspective on history, a disappeared lake may seem to be something like Alice's looking glass, the stuff of dreams and imagination. Yes, that which is tangible is lake bottom. But this shifting, "messy" Sumas Lake was shaped and encountered by living, experiencing bodies in the very real world. One can no longer learn to swim in Sumas Lake, but its past material reality permits other living bodies a chance to recover a sense of history and place. We interact with lake reflections that are not simply unreal or distorted: rather, the documents, photos, maps, and oral records are mediations, events of creation and translation, which continue to shape local stories and landscapes.

But why acknowledge the computer? Surely it is only a writer's tool and is not, in the study of history, immanent. But here I am trying to write an environmental history while immersed intellectually in theories and information technologies that appear to have the potential to push storytellers far from the nonvirtual (real) world where people actually chew vegetables and drink water. Now I am questioning the usage of drainage technology as I employ powerful computer technology, with enthusiasm and without question, to process words and search databases in order to replenish the lake with story. Paradox looms large and, to paraphrase Stewart Brand, "invention is the sincerest form of self-criticism."[10] I decided to produce a portion of my work in hypertext, "an information medium that links verbal and nonverbal information,"[11] in order to make visible and audible some of what I experienced in the creative process of historical research. My hypertext stack, made with HyperCard software, attempted to show how archival materials were convincing me, how existing photographs and maps, oral histories and narratives, were changing my ideas about the lake.

Despite my cautious beginning and my unfamiliarity with hypertext, this experience drew me towards the much-vaunted electronic frontier and made me more enamoured of computer technology than I had ever dreamed possible. Only my history books advised me to look around carefully. What was this heady world that was promising freedom and adventure? What did "pioneering" entail? A hard-copy examination of the relationship between the electronic and historical frontiers is not just a vain attempt to find a privileged place from which to survey the form of hypertext. The present work sticks close to shore. But how else can one critically examine the frontier and simultaneously communicate with people who have not yet been persuaded to go there, prefer to stay put, or cannot afford to go?

The result may be frontier advertising for new open space, but it comes with a large warning for would-be pioneers, a warning drawn from a recent work by students of the West: "Connections matter."[12] Even if the stories supporting the glorious frontier have been challenged, their consequences – the conquest of people and place – have been real. And now we seem to have the possibility of extending the stories visually, aurally, and textually. In effect, we may make them "hyper-real." But although hypertext can actualize and embody many exciting ideas of contemporary historical theory, new historical inquiry also serves as a refreshing critique of this much-hyped technology.

The word "opening" is evocative in the history of the West. With connotations of "empty" and "unoccupied," western Canada has long been interpreted as an open frontier, waiting for the presence and labour of colonizers.[13] Until recently, B.C. historians did little to change this notion. As Allan Smith notes of the major B.C. historian Margaret Ormsby, "Ormsby's general history gave [Indians] scant attention, and her 1960 appeal for new work made no reference to them at all."[14] This "sense of unoccupied timelessness"[15] persists, not only in the popular press but in the law courts where Justice McEachern judged a "vast emptiness"[16] to exist where the Gitksan and Wet'suwet'en beheld named and occupied homelands. If we privilege the written account and the "contact" experience as the beginning of the West, we re-narrate the discovery pageant and repeat the refrain that once earned me full marks in grade 10 social studies: "B.C. has lots of geography but little history."[17]

Strong resistance to the theory of historical emptiness comes from those who are increasingly sensitive to the legal and political context of Native history and who assert the anthropological and historical knowledge that British Columbia was neither empty nor timeless prior to newcomer occupation. Although the New Western History as a named genre comes largely from American historians of the West, who still tend to ignore Canada, the 49th parallel does not stop ideas, elk, air pollutants, or relatives from moving back and forth across the border. Scholars concerned with changing environments and First Nations are writing international history.[18] The open frontier was a shared myth, not simply in the sense of a falsehood but in terms of a story that for a time gave Westerners an identity and explained how they should interact.[19] For many, that particular story is no longer coherent, and we search for new openings into more powerful, more inclusive stories.

Some suggest that windows may be found in new conceptual structures. In *Under an Open Sky,* Sarah Deutsch urges historians to envision "an interactive multifaceted model,"[20] a framework more appropriate to diverse concepts of history. She does not speak of a technological solution, but following George Landow, who has written recently of the convergence of computer hypertext and literary theory, we may be tempted to see hypertext as the fulfilment of such requests for major renovations in historiography. Hypertext advocates such as Landow argue that we should stop thinking in terms of linear arguments, of hierarchies, centres, and margins, and instead should expand our vocabulary and mindset to recognize "mutilinearity, nodes, links and networks."[21] Hypertext, as conceived by the computer theorist Theodor H. Nelson in the 1960s, is "text that branches and allows choices to the reader, best read at an interactive screen."[22] Interactivity, diversity, choice – the buzz-words of new gender, ethnic, and class-conscious history – also click with the theory of hypertext.

The computer is familiar to many historians as an information-storage device and word processor, perhaps because they are prepared to characterize themselves as retrievers and processors of data. On the other hand, it is unfamiliar as a facilitator of creative and qualitative thought, not just because the software is new[23] but because historians, unlike students of literature, do not give themselves enough credit for being creative and qualitative creatures. My HyperCard stack is a variation on Nelson's nonsequential model. Although I have maintained a linear essay component, the "reader" is provided with opportunities to branch off to other materials, both visual and aural. Listening to recorded voices while reading my analysis may destabilize one privileged standpoint and add static to a monophonic authority. The ability to link to other materials formalizes multiple connections and allows complexity in a very messy West. The stack is cyclical, and because of the capacity to accept reader or additional writer comments, it is potentially open-ended. Emphasizing generation rather than reduction, the optimistic intention was to expand my understanding of Sumas Lake aided by others who might make new links and extend the "reader" fields.

The content of western history may thus interact with form. The very experience of reading hypertext becomes an exploration of the idea of westering. Like the men and women whom western historians write about, the "readers," given the opportunity and the tools, can "pick and choose between the known and the unknown," shaping the text, new goods, "new settlements" – an experience that can "carry with it an unexpected feeling of empowerment."[24] "Readers" can listen to recorded voices and privilege the slowing sensation of listening to other viewpoints and experiences of life. Or they can choose not to.[25] If the hypertext is formatted for the Internet's World Wide Web,[26] they can partake in the simultaneous remoteness and connectedness that has disrupted hierarchy in the West as they seemingly create, rather than inherit, the structure of their society. Most compelling of all, the software provides an open field for experimentation that is apparently limited only by imagination and computer power.

Early-twentieth-century pump technology offered agricultural science several thousand acres of Sumas Prairie on which to experiment; and thanks to hypertext, we have the opportunity to "discover" frontiers all over again. In an intellectual sense, the frontier was a new or unexplored area of thought or knowledge. Geographically, Sumas Lake was a frontier, lying along the border of another country; in fact, the Sumas River Valley extends into Whatcom County in the United States. In Richard Slotkin's mythical sense, the frontier "was the border between a world of possibilities and one of actualities, a world theoretically unlimited and one defined by its limitations."[27] The historical sense of Sumas Lake contains all these meanings, but it also insists that the "big opening" was a unique place, an ecosystem supporting communities characterized by conflict, interdependence, and interchange. As we define what we want from new openings, such as wealth, pleasure, or a new understanding, we learn that such places alter us as we change them.

This process may attune us to the dynamics of power, especially to the action of our words. When we attempt to rethink history by using the voices, images, or stories of others, the result may represent collaboration or exploitation, sharing or silencing. More likely, these materials will reveal both possibilities at once.[28] Hypertext may appear to offer a technological solution to bothersome authorial responsibility, but historians would do well to think again. Landow writes, "The main reason I think hypertext does not appropriate alien points of view, and thereby exclude them under the guise of pretending to include them, lies in the presence of the (politically) responsible, active reader: because the reader chooses his or her own reading paths, the responsibility lies with the reader. In linking and following links lie responsibility – political responsibility – since each reader establishes his or her own line of reading."[29] But ultimately, of course, the possible links and choices have been created by the writer. As the reader, you have the sensation of choosing, and if given the opportunity, you may respond, but you are aware that you are exploring someone else's moral universe. Freedom from creative responsibility is always a dangerous illusion.

The notion that serious problems of human relations are best solved by technical inventions (such as hypertext for cultural appropriation and IUDs for family planning) is hardly obvious. Just because a computer can do something like hypertextual history, we must not assume that it necessarily should. For storytellers who are concerned with the quality of place – the place of learning and the place of home – the opening provided by computers may be as enticing as an ozone hole.

At a 1994 hypertext conference, I was struck by the prevalence of geographical and spatial metaphors in the speakers' language. Hypertext authors were persuading us to enter new "environments," "landscapes," and "open space," to open up new "windows" as we sat in a dark, windowless, Barco-equipped hall. Experiencing the frontier through their fingertips, we were able to envision something which our awareness of the environment "out there" and the recognition of an historically occupied West advised us to stop dreaming about. Behold empty space for free unlimited discovery! Is the success of the propaganda dependent on some connection we are making between real environments and hyperenvironments? Or is it effective simply and ironically because a link to reality is no longer required? What might we be buying into? With so little sensory stimulation except what came from the screen and the speaker, we had become mesmerized by Edward Tufte and those who remind us that our brains can absorb great amounts of information and thus require the highest degree of resolution on the screen.[30] The more information you display, the more credibility you will have. The question "To what purpose?" tends to get lost in the persuasive novelty, which urges us to follow the prophets and open our wallets for further adventure to some place, any place but this, in this limbo of now.

In the worst scenario, we might wind up anywhere. Electronic media may have the potential to destroy that which is special about place and time.[31] If information from everywhere can be downloaded anywhere at anytime, what special knowledge will actual places – libraries, lakes – be understood to contain? Neil Postman warns that new technologies "alter the nature of community, the arena in which thoughts develop."[32] Certainly, when I first heard about Sumas Lake, I dramatically envisaged the disappeared body of water as a powerful metaphor for all the wrongs perpetrated on community by drainage and information technology. My deepest fears about the fallout from the global information explosion – cultural breakdown and erasure of local identity – were confirmed by my "discovery" of a disappeared and widely forgotten lake on the outskirts of my city. Admittedly, local history was not a strong component of my schooling inside classrooms in the 1970s and 1980s. But even now, as children learn more about the places where they live, through more diverse media, the forum of learning is inextricably linked to what we learn.

If, as philospher David Carr suggests, community is constituted by a shared story,[33] we should also be attuned to how computers can alter the way we transmit history. Lewis Mumford quotes the philosopher A.N. Whitehead: "Historical tradition is handed down by the direct experience of physical surroundings." But he adds, "Provided, of course, that these surroundings remain coherent and stable."[34] For some writers, the allure of hypertext has nothing to do with the offer of stability; its pull is more like the fascination of watching water swirl down the drain. As Michael Joyce describes it, we are in "flowspace." With the universal metaphor of water, hypertext is universalized. "Print stays itself; electronic text replaces itself."[35]

The (post)structural landscape may be shifting, but connections between words and things are still what must nurture us if our histories are to remain vital. The Hornby Island Official Community Plan begins with the idea that the "hardest nut to crack, of all the difficult nuts of environmental deterioration, is the very real human capacity to forget something not now present that was once of considerable importance to our lives, and the obvious inability to miss something we've never experienced. And so from generation to generation the environment becomes less interesting, less diverse, with smaller unexpected content."[36] Perhaps a solution to this human condition is not a costly simulation of what we are losing but a costly attempt to protect and preserve our real treasures, our real West Coast rain forests, our real water supplies – our real memory devices that link us, remind us, and reinforce in us the stories of the western past in a way that no computer can. These possibilities are not mutually exclusive; they involve our lives so that sometimes we must choose where we engage our time – and how we persuade ourselves to think about time.

Metaphors are often used rhetorically; that is, we may use metaphor to ensure the favourable reception of an idea by asserting that things we thought were difficult, unusual, or impossible to comprehend are actually very much like things we do understand. Not surprisingly, we often depend on spatial or geographical metaphor to discuss time, a difficult concept that may be easier to grasp with a tangible referent. Hayden White suggests that metaphor "does not give us either a *description* or an *icon* of the thing it represents, but *tells us* what images to look for in our culturally encoded experience in order to determine how we *should feel* about the thing represented."[37]

Time is a highway. Travelling from Vancouver on the Trans-Canada Highway over the Fraser Valley floodplain, we pass, in about an hour and a half, a fun park called Wonderland. This is not Alice's territory; we tail a Rabbit but it checks its rearview mirror not its pocketwatch. The strip malls, with their fast-food outlets, and services dedicated to the automobile become our local landmarks anchored to the open universe of international commodity trading. We are driving through what Brian Fawcett has called an "anti-memory device,"[38] wearing away a sense of place by telling us that we are any place. This is the true West, and you will be disappointed if you are seeking the romantic experience of visiting an abandoned ghost town. People drive to work here. We pass the lands of an Indian reserve and a band-owned brick factory; there, we view the products of a plastic pipe manufacturer; here, the artifacts of a gravel company.

We now travel on pavement supported in places by the Sumas lake bottom. Not too far along, we cross the Vedder Canal, which redirects a river that used to flow into the lake. The vista opens to the south past the green sod of golf courses – many tiny openings for little white balls in some of "the most fertile soil in North America," the "Green Heart of B.C." For the time being, we can rest assured that the lake bottom "proper" mainly supports dairy, hog, and poultry barns, sod farms, vegetables, neat and tidy rows, sturdy yeoman agribusinessmen, all reinforcing images of where we(?) came from, why planners were pushed to encourage hillside development, why the New Democratic Party of British Columbia created the Agricultural Land Reserve, and why the locals celebrate "Country Living Days." Good, honest, healthy living in open spaces. The lake bottom is now behind us, but the highway continues on; money too is time, and the billboards beckon, "Chilliwack is open for business. Phone the mayor."

Time could be an "information highway." Speeding down the on-ramp, we log onto an Internet node in Abbotsford called Sumas. It's an appropriate name; here is another kind of opening – another kind of innocent optimism, another territory to name and occupy. In an anarchic reordering of people and place, history may be debated in the unlikeliest of community forums. On newsgroup alt.sex.bondage, we read in somebody's post: "The Internet was started in the United States but has grown to be truly global in nature. Many people today join the Internet for the same reasons people came to America: freedom, choice, democracy, rich resources, opportunity to grow, room to expand, diversity on many levels, tolerance and respect of differences."[39] Just find a port of entry and begin.[40]

Maybe time is aqueous. In Halq'eméylem, the language of the Stó:lō, the tidal flows of river water may connect to concepts of both space and time.[41] Linear histories often impose on a river, and these projections are frequently imperial, contradictory, racialized, and sexualized. Is this river inevitably emerging from Eden, to flow past rurality to a fallen urban future?[42] Does the journey "back" take us to virgin, empty territory where the colonized (continuous with landscape) become irrational and prehistoric?[43] Fernand Braudel of the Annales school of history structured time as a fluid sea divided into depths, tides, and surface ripples.[44] Michel Foucault, on the other hand, argued that time is discontinuous but is connected in what as White points out, is the imagery of an archipelago, "a chain of epistemic islands, the deepest connections among which are unknown – and unknowable."[45]

Yet if time is not entirely continuous or made of such radically separated places, it might be a flood lake. Capacity overwhelmed, complacency disturbed, something goes and something stays, reminding us of links between past and future. If, as geographer Anne Buttimer suggests, water "lubricates, emancipates, renews and recreates human existence through time,"[46] a flood lake with both unpredictability and pattern might be like that time. We are in time as we are in space, and the challenge of a lake is that what has happened inside it is invisible to the casual observer.[47] Although the past retains mysteries and place, its particularity, Sumas might allow us to reinvigorate our relationship with time. To accept the invitation is to dive in, all senses open.

Our histories of the West can extend coherence and meaning to the environment, and this continuum can sustain us even though we deodorize the sensory realm, fill our ears with traffic noise, and reduce our positive metaphors of time to thoughts of highway distancing and material accumulation. Like any new opening to a way of seeing the world, we need to examine new technological openings warily. Something like hypertext may vitalize the creative practice of history. But as Howard Rheingold warns, "The late 1990s may eventually be seen in retrospect as a narrow window of historical opportunity, when people either acted or failed to act effectively to regain control over communications technologies."[48] To gain knowledge about our place in the world, to frame the answer to "Where is here?"[49] in the long term of inhabited territory, we need to explore time and place in ways that challenge our awareness and help our stories thrive.

Sumas Lake was, in the imaging of its drainers, a wasteland bypassed in the race towards modernization. We may now be drawn nostalgically to this image of Sumas Lake. However, we must not forget that one person's "margin" may have been a vital link in another's interconnected universe. Nostalgia may have us neglect relations of power and romanticize – museumize – past places and people. Thus, it is important to locate the deep end. Each of the following chapters represents a methodological opening to Sumas Lake, an exploration of the categorization of the lake through space and time in which my "I" is an active participant. "Listening for Pleasure" tests the waters, assessing lake values with the thoughts expressed in oral interactions. "Margins and Mosquitoes" plunges further into the paper documents of the archives, emphasizing links between histories local and national, vernacular and official. Emerging to encounter marshy rather than solid ground, "Memory Device" reflects on narrative traditions and the connections between place and the staying power of story. Then, in a monologue by this project's muse, "One More Byte" seeks to distance this project from the work of modernization while assessing the value of interactive history.

A question that students of environmental history must always confront is the relevance of history to the present. As I.G. Simmons asks, Is change so rapid that "all knowledge of all pre-existing conditions is obsolete?"[50] This question, unresolved, like that of Aboriginal title in British Columbia, must hang over the following discussions. The study of rapid change and the replenishment of desertified historical experience may well be an employment opportunity for tomorrow's historian. But an aim of *Openings* is to demonstrate that the honouring of place, no matter how changed, provides one positive opening for interconnected and engaged history. To honour is to question. History is in the books and mouths of storytellers, inside private homes, and in the public archives. History is also out there, and encountering and expressing it can be a process involving community, field, and lake work. *Openings* is a sharing of endeavours to move body and mind to care about local changes in the wider world.

Listening for Pleasure

Oral historians who focus their inquiry on a particular place may involve themselves in a messy enterprise. Oral history does not recover the unsullied story of the past. Furthermore, as Doreen Massey reminds us, "*places* have for centuries been ... complex locations where numerous different, and frequently conflicting, communities intersected."[1] In 1894 Sumas Lake stretched nearly twenty miles, touching the Sumas Indian reserves nos. 6 and 7 in the east and the fringe of the then-village of Chilliwack in the west. Thirty years later, was Eden destroyed or was wasteland reclaimed? Such a question, so weighted with value assumptions, reminds us that one does not begin an oral history project unaware of unequal relations of power or with the idea that questions will go unchallenged.

Recorded communications between individuals and groups, in both public and private spaces, then and now, are complex and sometimes discordant processes of cooperation, strategy, and translation. The notion of Sumas Lake as either wasteland or playland may be reinforced by the technologies of oral history – and, like photography, oral history is not simply about preserving "the way it really was" but is also a technique for gathering historical, rhetorical power.[2] Doing the oral history of a place like Sumas Lake includes the straightforward matter of asking people what they remember about it. But in order to articulate a larger domain of lake pleasures

Cousins swimming in Sumas Lake: Ida (Bowman) Campbell and
Clytie (Bowman) Greeno, *ca* 1897 (Neil Smith Collection [NSC])

Crew of the *Argo*, Orion Bowman's sailboat, on Sumas Lake:
Ida standing on the boat, Clytie seated, *ca* 1897 (NSC)

and possibilities, we might also begin to address already existing oral records with questions such as, Which people spoke? In which forum? And why?

Hoping to locate some orally transmitted lake knowledge, I chose to follow the relatively recent stream of oral history back to some documents that are neither typically linked to this methodology nor commonly connected to Sumas Lake. These transcriptions of testimony given to a government commission are not the products of oral history; but immersed within the context of the creative, engaged process of oral history, records such as these may help to enlarge and enliven Marc Bloch's definition of history: "a thing in movement."[3] Admittedly, oral history, with some notable exceptions,[4] is still located within a marginal area of the academy's activities, a zone flooded by local museum societies and enthusiasts. Many academic historians – like speculators gazing anxiously at the field during freshet – stake their claims on written documents, their semblance of solid ground. Yet on entering the adjacent field of anthropology, oral historians are encouraged to understand their research as being a fluid community process rather than simply material to be mined for fact and "preserved" by storage. Such an approach brings to oral history an awareness that the process of oral communication is not something that can be separated from nuggets of truth.

Interacting intimately with records, real people, and places, assumptions may shift, compelling us to confront the dynamics of historical construction. Furthermore, as Renato Rosaldo suggests, the identification of "our" stories becomes important as we explore "their" stories, looking for links between them.[5] Inspired by the arguments of feminist and socialist historians,[6] I hoped that attention to oral history would raise or salvage voices which dominant narratives had ignored. Yes, Sumas Lake had been drained, but that hardly proved that it and the surrounding floodlands were valueless to all the people who lived there. My own love of the nearby lakes, Cultus, Lindeman, Harrison, and Hicks, predisposed me to prick up my ears at any mention of lake value, particularly as a source of pleasure. A lake means "the beach," and it certainly means swimming. Despite my suspicion that popular notions of the beach would change a great deal across time, the photographs of families and groups of young people, often young women, smiling, swimming, and boating at Sumas Lake – snapped, of course, before the lake was drained – continued to feed synchronic notions of re-creational "Super Natural" British Columbia.

Only when, in my own oral exchanges and the oral records of others, I began to listen for indications of pleasure did my categories of Sumas Lake's benefits begin to blur. I did not locate the high ground where the "unprivileged" spoke for themselves; I was not reassured that oral history solely supports progressive and democratic agendas. But listening for value in that lake, I encountered descriptions of an enjoyed resource base that had not always been partitioned into useful and useless areas or into work areas and zones of leisure. The divisions that individuals make perhaps answer more clearly why the ecosystem was destroyed rather than why people lived with it. The oral record of Sumas Lake is extensive, and this study does not begin to be comprehensive. Rather, this brief discussion is an attempt to extend an opportunity to develop different interpretations and yet reflect a lake of potentially shared experience.

The oral histories of those who seek to rethink the past with an awareness of the First Nations sometimes contain the assumption that Aboriginal and white people can be portrayed only in opposing roles. As George Miles remarks of much ethnohistory in general, "The plots render Indians more interesting and important as foils for White history than as significant participants in it."[7] Oral histories involving Natives as interviewees may be subject to similar problems. Imbert Orchard's absorbing *Floodland and Forest* (1983) features the testimony of Stó:lō and non-Stó:lō people from the 1960s, gathered by theme into sound bites that reflect its original use in a CBC Radio series. We see none of Orchard's questions, but we can get some indication of his moral assumptions from his description of the area's first white settlers:

For them, it was a country without legend or tradition. They had left their ghosts behind them. A lake, however beautiful, was just a lake, a mountain a mountain, waiting for some surveyor to give it a name and measurement. A tree was just a tree – and probably in the way. As for animal life, they brought much of it with them, seeing it largely as a soulless commodity to be bred and slaughtered for profit. And whereas the aborigines filled their homeland with a throng of meaningful presences, white people, finding it was used only for hunting, fishing and gathering, simply saw an empty wilderness, awaiting the day when such as they would make it over – as a matter of right – in their own image.[8]

Orchard's description is a powerful indictment of the settlers, whose comments he has edited into generally celebratory passages about hardy and resourceful white

Sumas Lake, 1913, Miss Katie Walker and Miss Maitland (NSC, Klassen, *Yarrow*, 24)

The McConnell sisters, May and Myrtle, at Bellrose, July 1920
(NSC, photo by Jean Candlish)

men and women. If a book is an environment in itself, then his book has two separate spheres, focusing on separation rather than interchange after the fur trade era. Native people do not mingle freely with whites on the page. No Natives are given space to describe their stories of Sumas Lake alongside the edited memories of the white settlers.[9] Certainly, Native ideas are respected, but like a static museum piece, they supposedly take us "back into a very different world."[10]

Oral histories of Sumas Lake told by the white settlers of the Fraser Valley were created as early as 1945, when Major J.S. Matthews of the City of Vancouver Archives travelled to Huntingdon on the B.C. Electric commuter railway to interview Mrs Thomas Fraser York. The transcript does not list the major's questions, but York's transcribed answers show that she spoke of the "millions and millions of mosquitoes" on Sumas Prairie, "lots of deer, grouse and duck," and "the old Indian" who collected the mail for her family by taking a canoe across Sumas Lake, a man who "called himself 'Jim York' after us."[11]

The Chilliwack Museum and Historical Society and the Matsqui-Sumas-Abbotsford Museum Society (MSA) have been involved in collecting, transcribing, and storing local oral histories for over two decades. Here, in the spring of 1993, I began to listen to the questions of interviewers and to the entertaining answers of gifted storytellers. The tapes of Oliver Wells, an amateur ethnographer and a third-generation descendant of a local settler family, constitute a major record of Native oral histories, as does a 1987 compilation of his interviews with Stó:lō friends in *The Chilliwacks and Their Neighbors*. In the 1960s Wells could speak to men and women of Stó:lō heritage who had adult memories of the lake, people such as Mr and Mrs Kelleher, a couple living in Matsqui, west of Sumas Lake:

OLIVER WELLS: The draining of Sumas Lake made a difference in the country, didn't it?
MRS KELLEHER: Oh, my, yeah. My, we used to have a good time up on that lake, when we had the gas boat, and we'd get a crowd and go way up there to get out of the mosquitoes.[12]

While making history about a world that existed long ago, the question of who speaks for the oral record is largely determined by who is left to speak. In 1994 a person who recalled Sumas Lake as a young adult would be in his or her nineties. Edward Kelly, a Stó:lō elder who was born in 1900, spoke to Janelle Vienneau of the

Sumas Lake, 1901. A picnic party, and sail boat at Sumas Lake Ridge.
This photo was presented to the City Archives, 10 June 1945,
by Mʳˢ Thomas Fraser York, of Huntingdon, pioneer, of Port Douglas, Harrison Lake,
March, 1860.
City Archives. g.s.m.

Picnic at Sumas Lake, 1901 (City of Vancouver Archives [CVA], Out P-840, N-391)

MSA in 1987. He had spent some time at the lake as a child before being sent away to the Coqualeetza Residential School to be trained and Sunday schooled. His mother and father lived northwest of the lake at the Kilgard reserve (Sumas no. 6).

VIENNEAU: Well (laughs) amazing huh. What do you remember about Sumas Lake?
KELLY: Sumas Lake … I mentioned about the sturgeon and all varieties of salmon and trouts and the ducks were out there by the millions – way out, ducks and the geese. And the people had the small canoes in those days, and they – like for a Sunday outing – they would go out, like from the small slough into the big slough, then into the Sumas Lake and they would have a picnic, just family affair. I'm referring to my family. Mother used to make up the lunches and my dad would bring his rifle along and if we needed deer, he'd kill a deer. But the deer had to be down right near the water. If the deer was up a little, up on the side of the mountain he just won't … He just overlooks that deer because there's always deer all around. But the deer must be near the water before he would shoot it. Then he would bleed a deer and put his rifle away. And dad always brought his fishing line and dad would be trolling around up and down, mother would be knitting and us kids would be swimming in the lake. That's a Sunday outing.[13]

The childhood memories told to me include those of a man who cycled by the lake on an adventurous trip to Cloverdale[14] and a woman who went to the lake for summer vacations, where "we swam before breakfast, we swam before lunchtime – well, dinner at noon – we swam again in the afternoon and had a swim before we went to bed."[15] These two descendants of the first white settlers perhaps had more romantic images of the area than their parents. Speaking to Imbert Orchard in 1963, Mrs Fadden's daughter read extracts from her mother's journal regarding the flood of 1894. Mrs Fadden had lived at the far end of Sumas Lake for almost ten years. She was pregnant and had three small children, yet she wrote laconically of the expected high water – no panic. The day they started to build the boat, the water was "spreading over garden, over orchard, quite high. Fine day."[16] For the daughter, both danger and beauty were acute; that high water was "a beautiful sight. Wild roses used to bloom just at the top of the water. And there was the very lovely perfume that came from them as the water came up to them – a sight that was pretty, even though it was disastrous."[17]

As people spoke of Sumas Lake as a recreational spot, the persuasive visual images of lake pleasures were confirmed. But something else emerged in the oral interviews which the camera failed to capture. Many speakers developed the concept that the flood lake had provided an unofficial commons, the undivided space that in theory belongs to everyone in the community. Management was local, not national. As the writer Gary Snyder describes it, the commons is "necessary for the health of the wilderness because it adds big habitat, overflow territory, and room for wildlife to fly and run. It is essential even to an agricultural village economy because its natural diversity provides the many necessities and amenities that the privately held plots cannot. It enriches the agrarian diet with game and fish. The shared land supplies firewood, poles and stone for building, clay for the kiln, herbs, dye plants, and much else, just as in a foraging economy. It is especially important as seasonal or full-time open range for cattle, horses, goats, pigs, and sheep."[18]

Several men spoke about grazing cattle and sheep by Sumas Lake. People from as far away as Chilliwack brought their animals to feed on the grasslands at low-water time.[19] Kelly talked with Vienneau about this particular use of the lakeshore:

VIENNEAU: Would you know the value of the land when the lake was drained?
KELLY: The value?
VIENNEAU: The value, how much it would sell for.
KELLY: When I was a boy the land was one dollar an acre and my dad said when he was a boy it was fifty cents an acre. And the people were not interested in it because the people would say "why buy it? Why buy the land? When we could use the land for free?" Said, "there are no fences." The cattle, all the stock, ran out on Sumas Prairie. Say when my dad, now when it's milking time in the evening, would go out looking for the cows. The milk cows – if we see one cow we know our cows are there. And same with the horses, the needing any of the horses for any type of work, we would have to go out on the Sumas Prairie. If we see one horse we know our horses are there. Then for milking cows – my dad, when through milking, he would let the cows out of the barn. Then the cows would go out with the rest of the cattle and in the morning we had to look for them again.

Referring to the rules of the commons, Fred Zink spoke of the "gentleman's agreement" people followed in order to share the space and wild fodder peacefully.[20] No

Sumas Lake, B.C. 1905. Skating party on one of the swamps.
Orion Bowman, Mary Bowman, Ida Bowman, Nora York.
This photo was presented to the City Archives, 10 June 1945, by Mrs Thomas
Fraser York, of Huntingdon, pioneer of Port Douglas, Harrison Lake, March
1960.
City Archives. J.S.M

Skating party at Sumas Lake, 1905 (CVA, Out P-841, N-392)

one spoke of tensions or competing interests. In the interviews with white settlers, comments about Native people were rare and unsolicited, such as Charlie Power's remark about Sumas Prairie: "There was an Indian trail down there. They didn't bother us too much. They were pretty good."[21] Similarly, First Nations men and women rarely spoke of non-Natives. Yet the recreational area enjoyed by the local whites was also the beach enjoyed by the local Natives, and the Native fishing grounds were in the same lake in which non-Natives caught their fish. But this information was not on the same tape.

In these archived interviews, conflict was not mentioned (partly, perhaps, because the goal of the community history interviewers and interviewees was to create harmony). The "one-on-one" or "one-on-a-few" method of oral interviewing did not originate with oral history. But in its ideological attempt to widen the range of voices in history, the necessity of creating a comfortable atmosphere conducive to the establishment of trust and support has long been recognized. Since the widespread use of tape recorders and the blossoming of public history projects in the sixties, oral history has often been championed as the egalitarian method *par excellence* of creating history by and for the people. The sessions become feminist encounters, social and socialist meetings, "shored up by liberal amounts of coffee and cookies."[22] The memories that reinforce ideals of community cooperation are credible expressions in the friendly encounter provided by the serious excuse of history making.

For evidence of discord, I needed to look no further than the government commissions. The interviews conducted in hearings and royal commissions have often formed what oral historian Paul Thompson calls "a peculiarly intimidating form of interview, in which the lone informant was confronted by the whole committee."[23] Who speaks is a question not only of who has the right to speak but of who has the nerve to speak. Although the proceedings were often couched in polite or official language, I found that the Native-white conflict, which was so muted in the oral history interviews, formed a large part of the dynamic. For instance, in the government's bid to quell a farmers' threatened tax revolt after the lake drainage, landholders were called to testify before the agricultural committee of the Legislative Assembly of British Columbia in December 1925. Mr David Chadsey, a former dyking commissioner, was on the stand:

PATTERSON: You know the conditions as they are now; would you rather pay this tax, or would you rather go back to 2 years ago before the dyke was up?
A: I did not need the dyke, but I was public-spirited enough to vote for it so that the community would come under it, so that we could live, and not live like Indians.[24]

We go, then, to a forum that existed when Sumas Lake still existed; the context is provided by a watery place and by the historical background of government officials passing through, seeking a different order.

An oral culture created meaning in the Sumas environment for thousands of years before any European visited it and wrote home about it. In the context of colonization, fences and survey markers tangibly demonstrate the links between the spoken word, the written word, and things. Isabel Hofmeyr, in her study of boundary making in the Transvaal region of South Africa, suggested that fences " 'write' certain forms of authority into the countryside, and by representing the thin fixed line of the boundary in the earth, they imprint the textual world of maps, treaties, and surveying on landscape."[25] Fences are unnecessary intrusions for oral or paraliterate societies whose boundaries are more fluid and negotiable because they conform to a dynamic and seasonal landscape. Avoiding negotiation, invading powers could manipulate boundaries with the tangible authority of fence and paper.

In one extreme case, the colonial official Joseph Trutch disregarded oral instructions concerning the allotment of what he considered overly generous Indian reserve acreages in the Lower Fraser Valley of British Columbia. Oral communication for Trutch, even if delivered by a previous governor, was an "indefinite authority."[26] Like the settlers who moved into the valley, Native people could remove survey markers, and they probably did. But the markers were simply replaced, and in the Fraser Valley fences and survey lines remained "pervasive forms of disciplinary power, backed by a property owner, backed by the law and requiring little official supervision."[27]

Yet a lake is difficult to pin down. Flooded two months of the year, even the lands surrounding Sumas Lake were remarkably resistant to fencing and to accurately printed maps and consistent measurements. The lake and its marginal land was in the Railway Belt, and after Confederation, title was retained by the dominion government until 1924. Sumas Lake was not a cooperative feature of the new colonial possessions that translated easily into much-desired farmland. The idea of selling the

Edward Kelly at Sumas, 1912 (Matsqui-Sumas-Abbotsford [MSA] Museum Archives, P-1554)

Sunday school picnic at Bellrose Station, *ca* 1918 (MSA Museum Archives, N-512)

10,000-plus acres of lake bottom lands to recoup the construction cost of dykes had been in the pages of the Victoria *Colonist* as early as 1873.[28] But nearly fifty years later, people were still canoeing and sailing across the lake, and grazing cattle on its shores.

After the arrival of the Europeans, British Columbia continually blocked recognition and settlement of Aboriginal title. As of 1912, the federal government, though dissatisfied, remained willing to accommodate the province's intransigence. In September 1912, Victoria and Ottawa agreed to participate in the McKenna-McBride royal commission, the provincial-federal venture created to "finally adjust all matters relating to Indian Affairs in the Province of British Columbia"[29] – except that overriding concern of the Native people, title to their homelands and waters. The commissioners travelled for three years, from 1913 to 1916, visiting most of the places where Natives lived, hearing testimony, and making recommendations about land reduction and additions. Certain bands, such as the Kitwanga of the Nass Agency, refused to deal with the commission because their question of Native title could not be discussed.

In its attempt to forge a final solution to the "Indian problem," the commission failed badly. It lied to the Native people in stating that no reduction in reserve acreages would be made without band approval. Although the commission spent three seasons[30] in the New Westminster Agency, in effect it was just another visitor passing through. Like any other transcription of an oral exchange, the written record is no substitute for the real thing. The commission testimonies were certainly filtered and must be read with an awareness that not everything that was said was transcribed. A cynical approach to the commission records is therefore appropriate. Nevertheless, the statements of the men and women who chose to cooperate with the commission must not be dismissed today. The transcripts, reprinted by the Union of B.C. Indian Chiefs, constitute an important public record and confirm, in a written form privileged by a literate culture, that Native people were extremely concerned about what was happening to them and the places where they lived.

In contrast to the reluctance of First Nations people to jump on the commission bandwagon, groups of white settlers, boards of trade, and women's institutes were eager to have their opinions regarding appropriate land and water management considered. Their many ideas for reducing Indian reserves were based on shifting concepts of public pleasure as well as on private monetary gain. When writing about

Sumas Lake in flood, seen from the B.C. Electric tracks, *ca* 1912.
The lake lies beyond the treed Lakeshore Ridge (CVA, Out P-268)

pioneer perceptions of the West, Roderick Nash has stated that these newcomers did not love or aesthetically appreciate the wilds; they craved to destroy them: "They conceived of themselves as agents in the regenerating process that turned the ungodly and useless into a beneficent civilization."[31] Sumas Lake, surrounded by lush prairies and populated for centuries, though largely pre-empted by newcomers in the late nineteenth century, may not have fitted popular notions of "wilderness." Indeed, the established Native labour pool was integral to the success of the white settlers' "improvement" projects. Any contention that these workers were to move aside from their own territory to make room for ever more "improvements" required reinforcement at an official level to make dispossession legal.

At a meeting of the commission with the municipality of Sumas, the Farmers' Institute, and the Women's Institute on 11 January 1915, the white settlers asked the commission to release one of the Sumas reserves for a public park. Giving her speech the weight of an official written document and infusing the sort of "home front" rhetoric that found particular resonance in the midst of the First World War, Mrs Fadden read her petition aloud:

Our Motto is "For Home and Country." We feel like we would be taking nothing from the Indians that they really desire or need … It does not appear that their race will multiply to any great extent where this land would be necessary to them, and I am sure it is much better to have them all congregated in the one location at the mountain-side rancherie than to have these small holdings of land scattered here and there among the farms of the white settlers. They merely improve their farms to any extent – their habits of living are quite different, and their success as neighbors to us, I am doubtful to. Personally I have lived by this reserve land for over twenty-eight years, and I would enjoy seeing that tangle of underbrush and worthless timber removed, the valuable timber – which may be consumed by careless fire at any time – bring its value and a beauty spot created here in time, which would be an inspiration to many.[32]

The following day the commission moved on to the Kilgard Reserve (Sumas no. 6). The daughter of Old Man (Jim) York (who had worked for Mrs Thomas Fraser York) claimed title to the potential park, Sumas no. 7. She said, "The reason that land grew up again was because I only had one son and he has been an invalid for years."[33] York's daughter stated that she did not want anyone else to work the land. But the

Chief Ned (with cane) greeting visitors to the smokehouse, Kilgard, *ca* 1915
(Sumas Band Education Centre; MSA Museum Archives, P-1410)

hearings of white and Native concerns were formally separated, and Mrs Fadden's complaint about unsuitable neighbours went uncontested. Perhaps Mrs Fadden's Women's Institute might have retracted a request for this reserve if it had witnessed the testimony of York's daughter and York's wife, Ke Ha Jim. But perhaps not. The status of women was in a state of transition during and after the war, and as educated white women strove to define and demonstrate their own public worth as "civilizers", they simultaneously required a definition of the worthless and "uncivilized."

The male chief of the Sumas Band, Selesmlton (Ned), was called as the primary witness. A confident speaker, he attempted to establish his own agenda and his own standards of trust at the outset of the public hearing: "I am glad to see you people come into this house, and I am going to tell you the truth of what I am going to say."[34] Chief Ned went on to place the contemporary situation in a historical framework, noting the change over time and the reduced access to food resources: "That is the land and that is what the old people know, that is what they used to say. The Indians have always been poor, that is the reason I have always been worrying because I know the old people used to say that the White people will be shoving you around all over this open prairie to get our food, we used to get our meat, ducks and fish out in this lake [Sumas] and on the prairie." His words were statements of connection, reinforced and constituted by the surrounding territory, where his people made "half our living" from the "fish and ducks and things like that."[35]

In the process of ascertaining the band's success as agriculturalists in an area seen as prime arable land, the commission encountered farmers who had many head of cattle yet were extremely reluctant to transform places of water into places of land.

Q: Do you get plenty of hay?
A: We don't get hardly any timothy hay – we depend upon the wild hay.
Q: Could there be any land reclaimed here by dyking?
A: I could not say. I am against the dyking because that will mean more starvation for us.
Q: Why do you think that you would be starved out if this land were dyked?
A: Because the lake is one of the greatest spawning grounds there is and this dyking would cut it off and in that way would cut off our fish supply.[36]

The commission's inability to sustain relations of trust with Native people – rebuffing questions as basic as the chief's "I want to find out what is the meaning of this commission"[37] – is on record. Significantly, Chief Ned's word was not the highest authority to the commissioners, who tested his statements against those of the Indian agent the following month. This was a common practice, despite the fact that the Indian agents were not necessarily advocates of the ideas of those they were to represent; they asserted their own values.[38] For example:

Q: I suppose the wooded hillside and the portion of the land that overflows contributes largely to the feeding of their stock?
A: Yes, they depend upon the land on the Reserve for feed for all their stock. When the high water comes the low land is of no value to them and they have to shift their cattle up to the high land and they remain there until the water subsides, and two months after the water goes off the land it is possible to cut a fairly good crop of hay. The growth is very rapid and it is on this second growth of hay that they winter their stock ...
Q: About the duck-hunting – they complained that white men shot ducks there at night and sometimes killed the Indian's tame geese – the commission stated that the matter would be looked into – has anything been done in that respect?
A: In regard to men hunting in the night?
Q: Yes.
A: No. I have heard nothing further.
Q: Have they an Indian Constable on that Reserve?
A: No ... for the reason that I don't think there is any member of that tribe that would be suitable.[39]

Besides creating an undeniable record of Native dissatisfaction, the McKenna-McBride commission politicized Native individuals and groups. Andrew Paull, a translator for the commission, and the Reverend Peter Kelly became leaders of the newly formed Allied Indian Tribes of British Columbia, which worked to oppose acceptance of the McKenna-McBride recommendations and to forward claims to title as well as to water, hunting, and fishing rights.[40] At a meeting of the executives of the Allied Indian Tribes and the head of the Canadian government's Department of Indian Affairs on 7 August 1923, Peter Kelly asked, "Is it possible at all to get more lands, where lands are needed? And it is granted, I think, that in the New Westminster Agency, especially in Chilliwack Valley, Fraser Valley and the other parts of that

Beaver 2 tied up at Fook's Barn, Sumas Lake, *ca* 1905 (NSC)

Picnic on the shore of Sumas Lake, with Orion Bowman's sailboat *Argo*
in background, *ca* 1897 (NSC)

Agency, where people will be forced to make their living by agriculture – following agricultural pursuits, they will have to have more land if they are going to be able to compete with their white brethren at all."[41]

Kelly and Paull anticipated the negative response: only open Crown lands were available for additional reserves under the commission's terms of operation. The only time that Sumas Lake seems to have been mentioned at this conference was when George Matheson, representing the "Sardis group of Chilliwack Indians," defined his tribal territory in relation to the lake: "The Chilliwack tribal territory is right to Sumas Lake, that is the tribal territory, there was no boundary at that time, it runs beyond the boundary right down to Fraser River."[42] The lake was still a lake during the commission. But by the time the federal government had affirmed the McKenna-McBride report as the final adjustment of B.C. Indian affairs in 1924, the lake bottom had been transferred to the province, which quickly offered the land to private buyers.

Together with the Reverend Peter Kelly and their attorneys, Paull was ready to advance the cause of the Allied Indian Tribes all the way to the British Privy Council. In 1927 the Canadian Parliament averted this possibility by holding, in Ottawa, the "Special Committee Hearing to Inquire into the Claims of the Allied Indian Tribes of British Columbia, as Set forth in their Petition submitted to Parliament in June 1926." The extremely unpleasurable environment of this committee is evident even in the filtered transcript.[43] Integral documents were withheld from the Allied Indian Tribes, and the statements and demands of their chief consul, Mr O'Meara, were called "rot," "nonsense," "piffle," and a "scandalous waste of time."

Secretary Paull brought up the issue of water rights: "The reason the Indians claim foreshores on reserves in tidal waters is because the foreshore is just as necessary to the Indians as the reservation is."[44] Definitions were a major part of the debate, and one MP mused about the spatial ramifications of a foreshore: "Presumably what they want is the riparian rights and the water lots, whatever they might be, in front of the reserves. There is no such thing as foreshores on lakes; there might be, I suppose, between high and low water, but really the term does not apply to a lake or a river."[45] The B.C. Indian commissioner placed the idea in a temporal framework: "An Indian could not take up water in the olden days, and the commissioners did the best they could with the water allotments with the allotment of land. It was taken for granted that they had some value, but under the British Columbia Water Act these water al-

Canoeing in the dugout at high-water time; Mrs Michaud (*third from left*) with the Greenos and McAdams, *ca* 1919 (NSC, Lloyd Michaud)

lotments had no status whatever, and the only way an Indian can get water is by way of license under the provision of the British Columbia Water Act."[46] But this culture of argument regarding the value of both water and land to Native people – still in the early stages in the development of shared vocabulary and respectful conduct – was destroyed after the hearing. The committee found no factual basis for unextinguished Aboriginal title. Changes were made to the Indian Act which prevented Native people from seeking legal redress until the section was repealed in 1951.

Over the decades since the lake was made to disappear, comments about Sumas Lake have, as historian Joy Parr once wrote about a strike, "worn smooth, standardized in order, diction and cadence; shorn of dissonance in pursuit of a guarded social peace."[47] The History Circle of Euro-Canadian elders seated in Chilliwack's old City Hall repeated the descriptions I had already heard on archived tapes and in oral history books: lots of mosquitoes; good for duck hunting and picnics. When I privately posed the same questions to the people I had listened to on tape, I heard the same tone, sometimes the same words. Promising anonymity, I tried to work against the sympathetic, standard questions of interviews past. The result was silences, dissonance, disruption, and even a request to stop the tape – a request always fulfilled. Yes, a lot of pleasure, a lot of resources were gone, but emotions were mixed: it had happened long ago, and people had tried to adapt to the changes. The entire world had changed in seventy years, not just this one part of the valley.

Having read the bitter words of the commission testimonies, I returned to the process of interviewing people individually with a new awareness of personal and political ties to water and landscape. One Stó:lō elder, after speaking fondly of blowing across the frozen lake using his jacket as a sail, mentioned that in the 1920s he had used his car to drive political leaders such as Andrew Paull and George Matheson to their speaking engagements at local reserves, helping them "to help the people." He had no photos of the lake, but he began the interview by searching for the morning newspaper, excited by an article he wanted to show me. The front-page story regarding Premier Mike Harcourt's stop in Hamburg on his 1994 European tour began: "A prominent B.C. native leader tore into Greenpeace and the German people here Wednesday, accusing them of hypocrisy and of having a patronizing and romantic view of aboriginal people."[48] The elder wanted to know what I thought of the article before he began to speak about Sumas Lake. As the interviewee, I learned that the commons of Sumas Lake oral history remained alive and contentious.

B.C. Indian leader slams Germans, Greenpeace

KEITH BALDREY
Vancouver Sun

HAMBURG, Germany — A prominent B.C. native leader tore into Greenpeace and the German people here Wednesday, accusing them of hypocrisy and of having a patronizing and romantic view of aboriginal people.

George Watts stunned a packed auditorium of students, environmentalists and curious on-lookers as he launched a bitter attack on what he considered to be an extension of colonialism and paternalistic attitudes toward natives.

"That room flowed with hypocrisy," he said in an interview afterwards, his voice still shaking

■ MODEST SUCCESS, C20

with anger. "What they're doing is so damn typical. They're using Indian people for their cause. And they're going to be gone, and we're going to be left with all the problems."

Watts said his anger had been building for the past few days, as he took part in meetings between Premier Mike Harcourt and other B.C. government and industry representatives and German industry and political leaders, and as he watched constant Greenpeace demonstrations.

Watts was invited along on the trip by Harcourt. His expenses may be picked up by the government, but that has yet to be decided.

He said aboriginal questions have essentially been ignored during the trip by environmentalists and German industries.

"They're talking down to us. It's the same old story — we're going to tell you what's best for you, we created this mess for you and we're now going to create the solution," Watts said.

"I'm really amazed at how these people really think they're so goddamned right. I can't believe how sanctimonious they are with all their ideas and that. They have this romantic view of Indian people."

Watts, a former chair of the Nuu-chah-nulth tribal council on Vancouver Island and a leading native representative for the past decade, launched his attack during a debate at the University of Hamburg between Harcourt and environmentalists over B.C. forestry practices.

About 150 people squeezed into

Please see WATTS, A2

Vancouver Sun, 3 February 1994
(courtesy of Keith Baldrey, *The Vancouver Sun*)

Oral history is a place of mediation, where events are shaped and translated, where concepts of community and nature are generated. What provided pleasure at Sumas Lake? To my initial satisfaction, I located the beach. But pleasure was also about labouring, an activity that disrupts the romantic loss-of-paradise story, reinforcing the knowledge that both Stó:lō and non-Stó:lō people were agents of change, shapers of place and history. Without doubt, pleasure is about being listened to. Separating the voices of First Nations people and Euro-Canadians tended to silence the former and privilege the latter's "pleasure." To develop the potential of the oral record, whereby we avoid a simple condemnation or celebration of dominant narratives, we must find ways to expand its scope. Asking questions regarding the context of oral records can help open values to discussion. Certainly, any attempt to "mix" different voices may be linked to a fixation with racial categories and original Edenic purity.[49] And this too is open to question. Oral historians who attempt to span carefully maintained boundaries forged of politeness, silence, and tight essay structure do not do so because of their innocence or victimhood. Fully intertwined in the process, they can try to listen self-reflectively.

Margins and Mosquitoes

From the public archives in Ottawa, Victoria, Vancouver, Abbotsford, Bellingham, and Chilliwack to the private archives of band councils and private citizens, the repositories of Sumas Lake documentation contain, among their strong odours and their facts and fragile papers, some startling imagery. These representations of the unique and unusual, drawn persuasively in words, fill the imagination of the novelist and the scrapbooks of the antiquarian. But they also challenge the historian to value the local and the unique in a broader and more inclusive space-time framework.

John Keast Lord, an English naturalist on the International Boundary Commission that mapped the Northwest from 1858 to 1860, described a village out on the waters of the lake built by people he called "savages":

Endowed with an instinct of self-preservation, mosquitoes seldom venture far over the water after once quitting their raft – a fact the wily savage turns to his advantage. Rarely can an Indian be tempted ashore from his stage during mosquito time; and when he is, he takes good care to whip out every intruder from his canoe before reaching the platform. These quaint-looking scaffoldings, scattered over the lake, each with its little colony of Indians, have a most picturesque appearance. Fleets of canoes are moored to the poles, and the platform reached by a ladder made of twisted bark. To avoid being devoured, and to procure the sleep requisite for health, I used very frequently to seek the hospitality of the savages, and pass the night with them on their novel place of residence."[1]

Barbara Beldam (*left*) and Muriel McPhail (*right*) on the way to the
Chilliwack River lodge, 1921 (NSC)

One can also read the vivid descriptions of the rancher, horsewoman, poet, mother, and big game hunter Barbara (Bowman) Beldam, who was born on Sumas Prairie in 1904, the granddaughter of a surveyor who took control of land beside Sumas Lake in the late nineteenth century: "The vast warm waters of Sumas Lake were covered with thousands of wild ducks of every kind. Every evening they left the lake in large flocks to feed on the sloughs and pot-holes to the south. From the time I was able to hold a gun it was my greatest delight to ride out on the prairie and sit waiting by some slough for the evening flight. If I came home with three or four fat ducks how pleased every one was, and how good they tasted."[2]

The archives preserve boxes of letters, petitions, and engineering reports regarding the short, dramatic event – the elimination of Sumas Lake. But Beldam's duck hunting and the seasonal migration to the stilt village are events within a longer and equally relevant story – that of the living with Sumas Lake. Unable to write the ruin of timeless nature or to avoid the unresolved debate regarding Native land title in British Columbia, my reweaving of the other Sumas story into the land reclamation project is a somewhat risky narrative exercise in lake reclamation.

Sumas Lake was a community of creatures, making up one of the watery places on this misnamed planet. Rendered as a "drainage project," the story of the lake is easily absorbed into the international colonial theme of Western history, transforming local conditions into mere local colour. Again and again, outside powers have taken control of places and organized these new possessions to benefit and enrich mainly themselves (that is, "for the public good"). But on closer political and environmental on-site inspection, it can be seen that the old story is also – and probably always – new. Located spatially inside the Railway Belt of Canada, Sumas Lake was a national, provincial, and local concern. Positioned on a timeline of wetlands denudement, the drainage of Sumas Lake represents one of the major losses of wetlands along the Fraser River in the last century. But a delicate and complex web of relations links margin notes to attempts to marginalize people, links a British Columbian lake to some Great Men of Canadian history, and links mosquitoes to modernization. Tracing the web may help us reconnect the social and natural realms within which Barbara Beldam assures us that she was able to thrive.

MAPS AND MOTION

Beldam concludes a story of the Sumas area with a tone of frustration and a flat description of one of its archival traces – a map: "It is interesting to note that Sumas Lake, long forgotten by today's generation, is shown on a 1914 map of New Westminster and Yale published by the B.C. Department of Land and now unobtainable."[3] Unfortunately, even when individuals know where to copy maps in the public archives, the two-dimensional maps reinforce the prevalent idea that space is static, flat, and dead, unlike time, which provides life and richness to historical and geographic analysis.[4] Moistened with imagination and other archival resources, maps presenting synchronic spatial relationships may nevertheless be enlivened within an historical framework. But a map – a selection of geographic reality no more accurate than words – is perhaps a better place to begin than to end an encounter with a disappeared lake.

On looking at the International Boundary Commission map, we see that Sumas Lake connects with the Pacific Ocean, and thus with the Pacific Rim, via a river that empties into the Fraser. The map was made partly to assert authority over the area and the twenty thousand miners from the south who surged into the mouth of the Fraser in the spring of 1858, searching for gold. Sumas Lake felt the pull of the ocean tides and was part of the route and rearing habitat of migratory salmon and other international fish. Although Lord's subject was local, his description of the harvesting of "round-fish"[5] on Sumas Prairie was written in the romantic style popularized in Britain, a continent and an ocean away.

One may journey a long way to witness a prettier or more picturesque sight than Round-fish harvesting on the Sumass prairie. The prairie bright and lovely, the grass fresh green and waving lazily; various wild flowers, peeping coyly out from their cosy hiding-places, seem making the most of the summer; a fresh, joyous hilarity everywhere, pervading even the Indians, whose lodges in great numbers lie scattered about. From the edges of the pine-forest, where the little streams came out from the dark shadow into the sunshine, up to the lake, the prairie was like a fair. Indians, old and young; chiefs, braves, squaws, children, and slaves; were alike busy in capturing the round-fish, that were swarming up the streams in thousands: so thick were they that baits and traps were thrown aside and hands, baskets, little nets and wooden

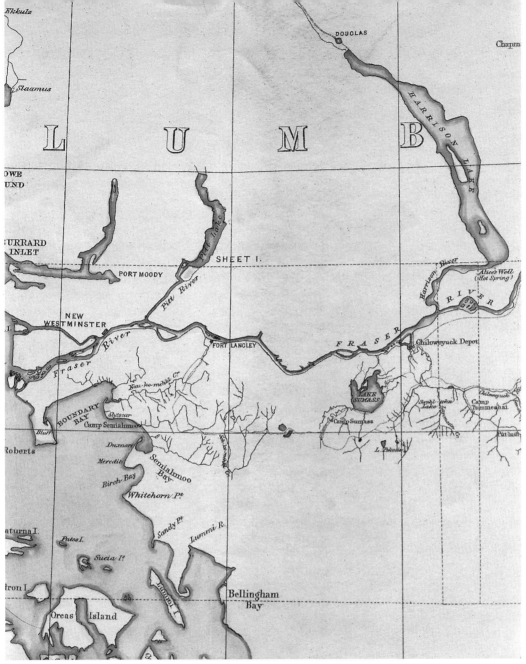

Map 1   International Boundary Commission map, 1869
Source: Royal Geographical Society, maps of the land boundary established by the
Treaty of Washington, 1846, sheet 1, index map, J.S. Hawkins

bowls did the work; it was only requisite to stand in the stream and bale out the fish. Thousands were drying, thousands had been eaten, and as many more were wasting and decomposing on the bank.[6]

In a map representing the time after the 1894 flood, the Chilliwack River takes over Vedder Creek and flows west as the Vedder River into Sumas Lake.[7] Plans to redivert the river into its northward channel were resisted strenuously by those whose farms were now safe from river action.[8] Students of Stó:lō history and geomorphology assert that the Nooksack River also once emptied into Sumas Lake.[9] The American end of the Sumas Valley in Whatcom County is eighty feet higher than the bottom of the prairie in British Columbia. The rising ground water levels and the flooding Nooksack periodically overflow into the Sumas Basin, unregulated by the Canada–U.S. Free Trade Agreement.[10] Perhaps we can envision the contours of this tense area of the international boundary and the furrowed brow of the mayor of Abbotsford.

The shape of the lake is rarely constant from map to map. Set in a very large time frame, such a variation in any lake is to be expected. All lakes are being filled in by sand, gravel, and sediments, and even without human or divine intervention, Sumas Lake would probably have become land eventually, filling up to the height of the Fraser River floodplain.[11] But this postglacial, perhaps ancient lake had some special features. For the people who occupied the region of Sumas Lake during the last 2,500 years,[12] the seasonal variations in the depth and area of the lake were events that changed their nature because of the way they related to them; as the local inhabitants innovated and adapted or periodically moved, the freshets could be understood as blessings or threats. Before the drainage commenced, Canada's resource inventory team, the Commission of Conservation, regarded the lake as something to measure. Its members did not attempt to conserve the lake, but during their brief visits their premortem examinations of the body of water related that it was nine feet deep at low water and thirty-six feet at extremely high water.[13] Deeper than the high-altitude Lake Myvatn in Iceland (famous for its diverse waterfowl population) and with much less variation in area than the flooding and evaporating Lake Chad in West Africa, Sumas Lake was – and the lake bottom still is – situated close to sea level in the floodplain of several North American rivers.

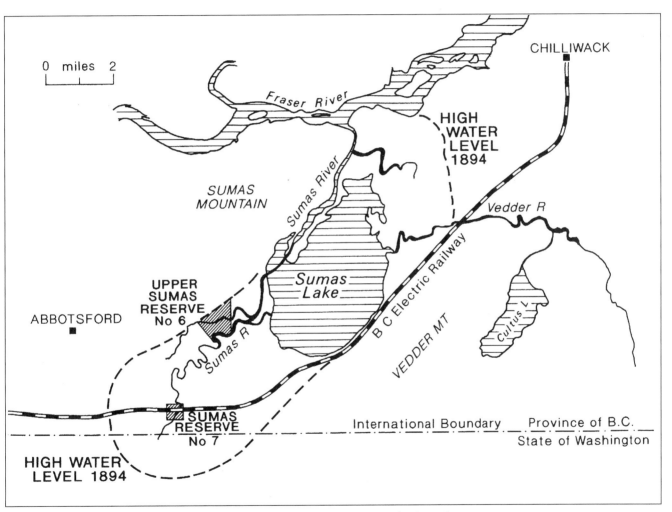

Map 2   Hydrographic Survey map, 1912 (redrawn)
Source: National Archives of Canada (NA), RG89/533/841

Space need not become the fixed surroundings for the tale, as lifeless as a section setting the stage, full of forgettable descriptions of flora and fauna that rarely intersect with the action to follow. The environmental historian William Cronon counsels, "Any geographical description, no matter how static, can be set in motion by asking: how does this place *cycle?*"[14] Such a question might reanimate the century-old specimens of Sumas Lake birds and mammals in the Museum of Vertebrate Zoology at Berkeley, California,[15] might reduce the stings of mosquitoes to a seasonal, intermittent experience, and might render Sumas Lake not as part of pristine, timeless wilderness, but as a human resource base in the Pacific flyway of migratory birds that was showing signs of strain before the turn of the century. An examination of documents concerning the first attempt to dyke the Sumas area and drain the lake links the federal and provincial governmental powers to the agency of a local ecosystem.

DEFINING THE MARGINS

The margin depends not only on who is doing the defining but also on when it is defined and why. In economic terms, marginal land is "land so poor as to remain unused until the lack of more desirable land forces its development."[16] Desirability is, of course, a relative concept, but certainly a lake and its surrounding wetlands are poor land. I.G. Simmons's environmental history text defines wetlands as a marginal landform "where the substrate is subject either to periodic (diurnial, seasonal, unpredictable) or permanent inundation."[17] Because the wetlands covering approximately 6 per cent of the earth's land surface[18] are generally dispersed in relatively small areas, conversions of these places to land by people – often for profitable agricultural purposes – remain attractive though open-ended projects. Wetlands around the North Sea have been claimed for centuries,[19] though because of the soil wastage after drainage, areas such as Britain's Fens must be pumped ever more vigorously.[20] Thousands of acres of wetlands have been destroyed more recently through dyking and drainage in British Columbia's Lower Mainland.[21] Without its powerful pumps transforming the "margins" into valuable agricultural land each year, Sumas Lake would begin to refill its old lakebed as it did when the dykes burst and the pumps could not handle the flood in 1935, 1951, and 1975.

The human experience of Sumas Lake shifted profoundly with the changing seasons. Records of certain short-term observers provide an insight into a range of local activities that varied as the earth changed its position in relation to the sun. Winter temperatures in the Fraser Valley seem to have been irregular.[22] The journals of Fort Langley report a relatively mild November in 1828. On the fifth, the Hudson's Bay Company employee François Noël Annance (a Métis nicknamed "the Scholar") and his party navigated up the Sumas River, where they found "300 or 400 Indians of the different tribes from this neighborhood encamped – leaving them, taking a couple with him as guides, he continued a short distance through a large lake."[23] Annance left hurriedly, for the villages were preparing for an attack from a coastal tribe, and he returned to the fort with two beaver from "the Indians at the Lake." The weather was rougher during their return journey in December, but the rivers remained clear: "Their course was up the main river for about 25 miles, and ascended the Smoise [Sumas] River the distance of about 5 miles; when they arrived at a Lake of 10 miles long and 6 wide [Sumas Lake] – at the extreme end of this lake they found a considerable extent of low clear country, intersected with a number of little creeks & ponds well adapted for wild fowl – here they spent the best part of three days, and killed 4 Swans – 3 Cranes – 10 Geese & 40 Ducks."[24]

As Sumas Lake receded to its lowest water level, floodwater mosquito eggs dried out and passed the winter waiting for the good chill that would allow them to hatch in the summer. Charles Wilson, another member of the boundary commission, recorded in early November 1859 that everything was frozen: "We have to thaw our bread over the fire before eating it, beef, vinegar, ink all the same way."[25] They adopted the local custom of wearing blankets. Communication both on the river and on the page became difficult during a freeze-up. At Camp Sumass, Wilson wrote, "The process of thawing the ink is to stick your pen into your mouth after every 5 or 6 words and keep it there till it thaws."[26]

Although the work of reorganizing nature was advanced by the Protestant and Catholic ethics that began to dominate the area in the nineteenth century, the identification of the nonhuman at Sumas Lake was also aided by men of science such as the naturalist John Keast Lord. He made several observations about the wildlife of the Sumas area in notebooks that are "punctuated" by the squashed remains of several mosquitoes (which were recognized by later entomologists as the dominant floodwater species *Aedes sticticus* and *Aedes vexans*).[27] Understanding himself and his mission of documentation to represent a radical break with the Aboriginal people he encountered, Lord freely mingled descriptions of Native life with those of the insects and animals he was studying. Reporting on the life cycle of the mosquito, he noted that the eggs were laid on ground that was due to be flooded or in small "canoes" on water.[28]

Lord and Wilson each declared the Sumas-Chilliwack area to be "a Second Eden," and despite the mosquito menace, which drove the greatly distressed Wilson to sleep with a dozen men, women, and children "in the middle of the lake upon piles ... after smoking no end of pipes of peace" with the chief,[29] both men registered claims for land in the vicinity.[30] They saw lush grassland, suitable for grazing cattle, that was "rapid beyond anything I have witnessed elsewhere," growing in two months to a height of "four and seven feet."[31] Today, the grasslands of the Fraser Lowland are almost completely gone, and thus it is difficult to identify the species that astonished the surveyors. But before the lake was drained, "wild" grasses were still being harvested by local farmers. Barbara Beldam reflected, "I believe Canadian blue-grass to be the most undervalued of all grasses; when the waters receded it sprang instantly back to life so that there was always time for a good crop of hay. I have seen droughts that Canadian blue-grass has taken in its stride, cowering under the sun until the first rain brings it back, green and eager again."[32]

Lord was recording an abundant and well-used food resource as the ospreys and bald eagles fished in the lake with their claws. The anthropologist Wilson Duff, in his fieldwork of the 1950s, described a weir which then existed across the Sumas River at the point where the river left the lake at a width of two hundred feet and a depth of up to twenty feet. The weir was owned by the Sumas people, but they allowed outsiders to use it; they opened it after they had caught what sturgeon they wanted.[33] The wild potato, *xwoqw'o:ls*, the wapato or arrow-leaf, was gathered around the shores of Sumas Lake and provided a good source of carbohydrates whether eaten raw, boiled, or roasted.[34] The Nooksack, who today live south of the imposed border between the United States and their relations in British Columbia, came up to use the lake's west and southern shores for hunting and fishing; if they wanted to make sinew-backed bows, they could obtain sturgeon glue as well.[35]

Lord wrote of the numerous birds that arrived, "as if by magic," to devour the insects as their numbers grew in summer.[36] These birds included flycatchers, white-bellied swallows, and sedgebirds (warblers). Sumas Lake was also attractive to sandhill cranes, great blue herons, and American bitterns.[37] Lord hunted the birds he listed, and he was particularly annoyed by the "disagreeably bold" behaviour of the bald eagles that flew off with his kill; sometimes he gave a robber "the benefit of a second barrel, as punishment for his thievery."[38] "Immense flocks" of the now rare white-fronted goose, as well as whistling swans and Hutchin's geese, also spent part of their life cycle at Sumas Lake.

Lord was hardly alone in the hunt. One way the locals captured birds was to string nets between poles that were fifteen to twenty feet high, each of which was attached to a canoe, with which they would slowly enclose a roft of ducks.[39] With the improvement of guns in the nineteenth century and the increasing trade in them and use of them, hunting methods changed. Lord described how some unnamed Natives used firearms in hunting white-fronted geese: "They arch light sticks by fixing the ends in the ground, just high enough for a man to crawl under, and about six feet long; this they cover with grass, to resemble a mound and rushes; having crept in, the Indian lies still until a flock of geese pitch within shot; then, bowling over as many as he can, he loads again; the geese just circle round and pitch as before, and so he continues to fire until enough are slaughtered; then out he creeps, to pick up the dead and wounded."[40] The wary white-fronted geese were already seriously reduced in number by 1888.[41] Hunting seasons and bag limits were to be a new concept for some hunters, including the increasing crowds of newcomers whose object in the hunt was often to kill as many birds as possible.

Before long, short-term visitors began to stay for the long term. Migrants such as the Chadsey brothers moved into the lake country not long after the colony's Pre-Emption Act of 1860, which granted 160 acres of unsurveyed Crown land to those who would take possession, pay the small sum of ten shillings per acre, and register title. In 1864 William McColl surveyed Indian reserves between New Westminster and Harrison River. According to the oral instructions of Governor James Douglas, all lands claimed by the Indians were to be included and in no case was a reserve to be less than 100 acres.[42] The government engineer mapped the area at the beginning of freshet season, and he noted that the two Sumas reserves (Lower Sumas with 6,400 acres and Upper Sumas with 1,200 acres) were both mainly flooded at high water.[43] Three pre-emptors had already moved onto the Lower Sumas Reserve, where McColl listed a Native community of ninety-three people.

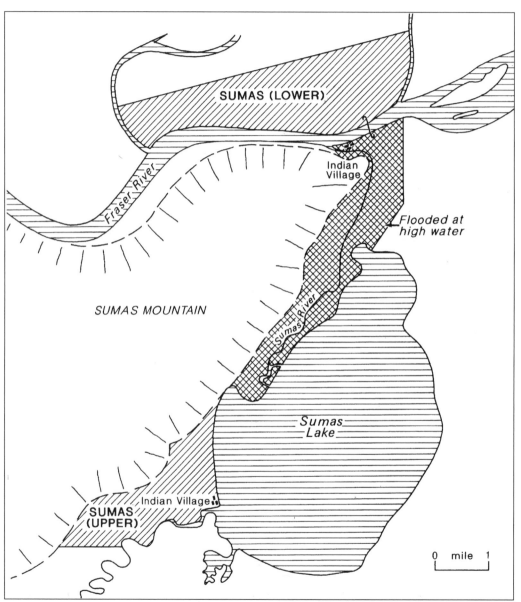

Map 3   "A Rough Diagram Shewing the Portion of the Reserves Laid Off for Government
Purposes on the Fraser, Chilukweyak, Sumass and Masquee Rivers," 16 May 1864 (redrawn)
Source: British Columbia, Surveyor General Branch, land reserves drawer,
plan 31, tray 1, W. McColl

In 1867 Joseph Trutch, chief commissioner of lands and works, acted to reduce the size of the Lower Fraser reserves, arguing that "the Indians regard these extensive tracts of land as their individual property; but of by far the greater portion thereof they make no use whatever and are not likely to do so; and thus the land, much of which is either rich pasture or available for cultivation and greatly desired for immediate settlement, remains in an unproductive condition – is of no real value to the Indians and utterly unprofitable to the public interests."[44]

Trutch proceeded to allow 40,000 acres[45] to be made "available" by taking it from people he had once compared to dogs.[46] The surveyor sent that year to carry out these reductions reported, "In our reconnaissance in the Chilliwack District [east side of Sumas Lake] we were accompanied by nearly all the settlers, some sixteen in number, who were very useful and obliging in pointing out ... surveyor's posts."[47] As the political scientist Paul Tennant has noted, the surveyor was innocent of any suspicion that the settlers might have previously moved the posts they knew so well.

Although the white settlers were still in the minority in the Fraser Valley, they were Trutch's "public interest." Between 1861 and 1871, their numbers grew from 300 to 1,292.[48] By comparison, even though the imported smallpox virus was killing many Native people in British Columbia during this period, the Stó:lō numbered at least 1,720 in 1864.[49] Some government outsiders were more sympathetic than others to the Sumas who were so actively being separated from their territories. Surveyor J.B. Launders, for instance, was unable to satisfy some very disraught Sumas Band members within the scope of his surveillance duties. Sumas no. 2 on the Sumas River,[50] he noted, was "chiefly wet prairie with a belt of stunted willows along bank of river. The Indians were not well satisfied: they wanted all their original claim."[51]

After British Columbia joined Confederation, the province and the dominion had difficulty merging their conflicting policies towards Native people. Stó:lō grievances filled numerous petitions.[52] The province's refusal to recognize Aboriginal title and its reluctance to enlarge the existing reserves led to the formation of the Joint Allotment Commission in 1876.[53] Three commissioners were given the task of conclusively settling the land question for British Columbia. Band populations were noted as well as individuals' names, numbers of livestock, and implements.[54]

By 1878 Gilbert Sproat, the most enthusiastic member, was the only commissioner left on the job. Before joining the commission, he had been absent from British

Columbia for nine years, but his observations on B.C. Indians during his earlier years in Alberni show him to have been a remarkably thoughtful settler.[55] The geographer Cole Harris has described how Sproat met with the Lower Fraser chiefs in 1878 to hear their complaint that incoming settlers were claiming land which their people wanted, but nothing was being done to remedy the situation.[56] Harris is correct in saying that the situation remained dire. But Sproat's lengthy written attempt to argue for fairness is a story that has special relevance to Sumas Lake, for it magnifies the interdependent relationship of its water and ground. After passage of the Sumas Dyking Act that same year, the unsatisfactory situation for the first inhabitants of the area worsened.

Engineer Edgar Dewdney was one of the first to survey the Sumas district and suggest draining the lake.[57] In April 1878 the first legislation relating to Sumas was written and adopted, enabling Ellis Luther Derby "to drain Sumas Lake and other lands" in the Chilliwack, Sumas, and Matsqui districts.[58] Derby did not begin construction until November, waiting perhaps for low water. Then, just after Christmas, he received a dark warning from Gilbert Sproat:

To E.L. Derby   Dec. 26, 1878
Sir,
I have to inform you that it is the intention of the Dominion Government to take legal steps against you as a trespasser upon the Indian Reserve at this place and to restrain you from further similar proceedings with respect to Indian reserves at Sumas and Chilliwhack.

It is considered that the Sumas Dyking Act cannot give you any authority to touch Indian Reserves, that can be given by the Superintendant General of Indians alone acting with the consent of the Indians.

I have the honour to be Sir,
                              Your obedient servant,

                                                                                    Gilbert Malcolm Sproat
                                                                                    Commissioner[59]

Derby protested,[60] and Sproat countered with a volley of angry letters. Sproat apparently had sent a letter of protest against the Sumas Dyking Act the previous spring, but he noted that such a letter would hardly seem necessary in view of the province's knowledge that the lands in the Derby grant had not been examined by a reserve commission.

Authorized by the Act, Derby began his dyke in Matsqui and planned to run it across a Sumas reserve. All the Crown lands near the Matsqui, Sumas, and Chilliwack reserves had been granted to Derby by the provincial government, and Sproat was outraged that the question of "sufficiency of these reserves" had thus been resolved.[61] "Derby now pleads that the general effect of the dyking could be beneficial to the Indian reserves," protested Sproat, but the crucial question remained. How could sufficiency be judged when every acre of Crown land beside and near the Indian reserves had been granted to Derby?

Sproat challenged Ottawa on behalf of the Matsqui people, who "had been told by white men that if they or their cattle injured the dyke they would be put in prison." The people felt not only that the dyke was useless but that the reserve was unsuitable, he said. "The effect of draining lakes and diverting the course of streams touching or near the Indian reserves has also to be considered: in short, the whole question pre-eminently requires the well considered sanction of the Dominion Government and requires it now."[62] For the short-term stay of Sproat, the time to act was slipping away. He thus recommended the disallowance of the Sumas Dyking Act.

British Columbia's chief commissioner of lands and works, George Anthony Walkem, wrote to Sproat telling him to drop the issue, and in a telegram he assured Prime Minister John A. Macdonald that he would "immediately protect Indians from contribution for benefits by an ammending act."[63] Walkem's record with regard to Indian interests was hardly exemplary. As premier in 1875, he had opposed the motion to publish all papers relating to the Indian land question and in the end had succeeded in suppressing the report. Sproat had agreed to continue as the sole reserve commissioner only after being assured that the chief commissioner of lands and works would not interfere in his work except in extreme cases.[64] Yet Walkem continued to do so, writing to Ottawa to provide "some important facts" and saying that he had it "upon good authority" that the land under the lake was "a rich loam" and that its value, to Indians as well as whites, would be increased by drainage.[65] Again, he asked that the Act, which could be disallowed by the dominion government before 8 May, continue to stand.

As so often happened, the question of land sufficiency for the Indians remained open because of seasonal considerations; Sproat was unable to answer the question in

To G. M. Sproat Esq   3 April   187

Indian Reserve Commissioner

New Westminster

British Columbia

Proceed at once to Chilliwhack,

Sumass and Matsqui – Ascertain

if Reserves sufficient – when drained – if not

what further required and

report the result by telegraph

charge Indian Branch

L V K

Telegram from Lawrence Vankoughnet to Gilbert Sproat, 3 April 1879
(NA, RG10/7538/27150-8-20)

January because of the snow on the ground. He was instructed to "proceed at once to Chilliwack, Sumass and Matsqui – ascertain if Reserves sufficient, when drained, if not what further required and report the result by telegraph."[66] Strangely, the words "when drained" were added as a marginal correction on the telegraph. In a letter to the prime minister the same day, which described the instructions to Sproat, the concept sufficient "when drained" was omitted.[67] The May deadline passed and the Sumas Dyking Act remained in place.

Surveying in the June freshet of 1881, Captain W.S. Jemmett noted willows, crabapple, fir, cedar, maple, hazel, vine maple, berry, fern, spruce, alder, and grass on the Sumas Reserve (no. 7). As the handwriting in his field book became messier and messier, he also noted more than three feet of water, hardhack, a beaver dam, a swamp, and unearthed survey markers.[68] As early as 1879, the sufficiency of land for Indians in the Lower Fraser was tied to a drainage scheme that cyclically stopped and restarted for the next forty years as white farmers argued and as capital remained elusive. Although Sproat raised the possibility that lake drainage might not be in the best interests of the Native people, the debate was cut short. He stated that the Indians "must have winter and summer grazing land … reasonable area and their fishing places," and he asked, "Is this unreasonable for a law abiding people whose land title is inextinguished?"[69] But the dominion, the fiduciary guardian of Indians, was mute. Sumas and Chilliwack Natives would not have to pay for drainage or dyking; but Indian agents would thereafter assume that the Indians, on their increasingly tiny pieces of dry land, not only favoured but required drainage.

The Railway Belt, twenty miles on each side of the promised Canadian Pacific Railway, was transferred from British Columbia to the dominion in 1883; but in 1896, 45,000 acres of the "Sumas Dyking Lands," excluding Sumas Lake, Indian reserves, and certain "marginal" lands, were reconveyed to British Columbia to facilitate the administration of settlement.[70] The 1884 lynching of Louis Sam, a fifteen-year-old Sumas boy, by U.S. citizens in cooperation with white Sumas Prairie residents indicates that the relationship between Natives and newcomers was strained.[71] The great gray owl stopped coming to Sumas Prairie in the winter; other birds of prey, the gyrfalcons, became the prey of market hunters. New settlers occupied most of the available agricultural land by 1888,[72] and successive dyking commissioners felt justified in urging a revision of the amendment that "unfairly" prevented the taxation of Indians for dyking projects.[73]

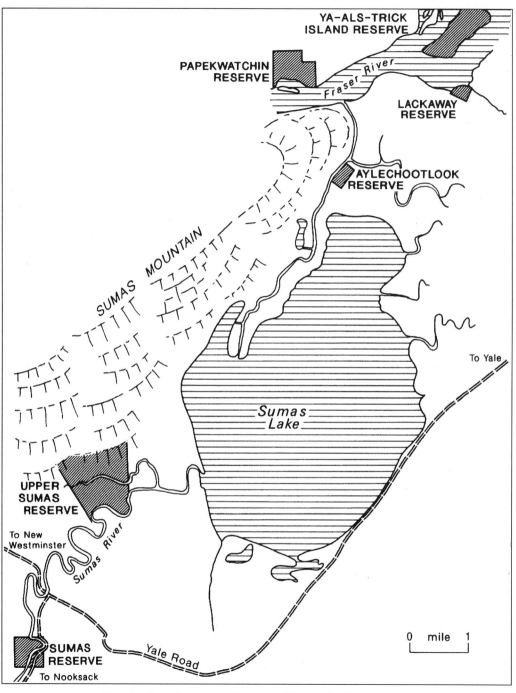

Map 4   Captain Jemmett's plan of Sumas Indian reserves,
New Westminster District, 1881–82 (redrawn)
Source: Energy Mines and Resources Canada, Legal Surveys Division, CLSR plan no. BC253

But apart from any discussion of land rights and use, let alone actual control of water and land, Indians could be portrayed by white settlers quite approvingly. Charles H. Evans, a farmer who grew up in the area, wrote in the local paper in 1904 of the "Fraser Indians" as they appeared to him in the latter half of the nineteenth century:

The only obtainable help at that time was the Indian. He was the pioneer's live capital. He was the man who cut down the bush and the trees. He cleared all those first fields; he helped cut the hay and grain that grew on them. He baled hay, made roads and bridges, and did all manner of farm work. In some cases the rivers were our thoroughfares at that time. The Indian took the produce down the streams to the Fraser, where he could have it loaded on the steamer. Large or small, he could take it just the same in his canoe, and sometimes for heavy articles two or three canoes side by side. He was always reliable.[74]

In the early twentieth century, the same farmer seems to have employed the services of a growing number of migrant labourers and local farmers, both Asian and white, much more often than the "reliable" Indian.[75] The Indians to depict favourably were the Indians of the past – not the contemporary holders of valued land and competitors for resources. But certainly, qualities of sensitivity and insensitivity may coexist in one person.

In Beldam's poem "The Return of Chief Sumas" the Sumas Indians have disappeared completely from the valley, struck down by land dispossession, alcoholism, and disease. The chief, on returning from the spiritual realm, remembers the valley and is horrified by its present reality: "O my Father, I am ready to return unto my people, I have seen my old-time homeland / but the land is mine no longer, for the great white hand has killed it. / Once the Garden of My People, it is now the White Man's Burden / I will leave it now forever …"[76] Beldam recalled that her father, W.C. Bowman, sheltered two families of Indians in a driving north-wind storm and froze his cheek and some toes in the process of saving their team.[77] She did not note, however, that her father was also a dyking commissioner who travelled to Ottawa to advance the drainage scheme. In 1910 he complained to the Department of Indian Affairs that the existing reserve land was "practically unused," he said that the "Indians were diminishing in number … not suited for intensive farming," and he suggested that they be confined "in as small an area as reasonable and possible."[78] Out of sight and out of mind – a timeless and empty place perhaps shared, in this wild settler fantasy, with attendant bits of troublesome nature like the mosquito pest.

MOSQUITO RHETORIC

Regardless of what local or federal officials had in mind for the Stó:lō and the lake area, neither of which had disappeared by the First World War, they had clearly defined plans for mosquitoes. Most information written about mosquitoes has been gathered with the intention of eradicating them. For instance, before the lake was drained, *Aedes aldrichi* (*A. sticticus meigen*)[79] was the most significant species in the Fraser Valley in terms of abundance and vicious biting behaviour towards mammals, especially in the evening, though *Aedes vexans* was the most important mosquito for entomologist mammals near Sumas Lake itself.[80] This species still irritates many people in the Lower Fraser Valley around July, and usually it is considered to be the worst mosquito pest in Canada. No malarial outbreaks are known to have occurred in British Columbia; the only disease carried by indigenous mosquitoes is encephalitis, which on rare occasions has been known to affect horses, people, and wild rabbits.[81] In the perceived war between human and mosquito, mosquito science is not neutral. Nevertheless, the rhetoric of science and the laws of nature produced by entomologists offered a persuasive means of plucking the drainage debate from the fabric of Sumas society. The scientific remedy of drainage, promoted intensively after the First World War, produced new knowledge as it helped to destroy wetlands – and a way of life – in the Fraser Valley.

The locals had long developed mosquito-coping manoeuvres. Although the platform houses seem to have been out of use by the late 1860s, smudge fires remained important. A surveyor on the International Boundary Commission was soothed by a Native woman's application of vermilion onto his face and hands. The Stó:lō historian Dan Milo spoke of *t'ehm-eh-ĸwɪʏ-ehl*, an important campsite east of the lake where the Stó:lō came to get away from the mosquitoes.[82] Later, the locals put screens on windows, swished themselves with sticks, applied creosote to the walls and repellents, such as oil of lemon grass and lavender, to their skin. Packaged relief was sold at the drug store. Common control measures included pouring crude oil on mosquito breeding areas, a practice detrimental to fish and fowl as well as insects. Some people, women especially, could simply work indoors. As a young person, Ms Bellrose spent a considerable amount of time inside the family house by the lake all year round. Her diary of constant indoor chores and her daughter's oral reflections on the loss of a "scene" and a "view" rather than a lake reflect a domestic existence[83] – a stark contrast to the experience of Barbara (Bowman) Beldam, whose hunting and horseback riding enabled close and regular contact with the outdoors.

Beldam writes: "How glorious it was when spring came, and how short! For, with warm weather came literally clouds of mosquitoes, especially if it was a flood year. My sister and I wore long black stockings lined with paper. Heavens! No girl wore pants in those days! The haymakers wore big straw hats with mosquito-netting veils that could be suffocatingly hot. All the animals suffered but particularly the horses. I remember running my hand down my horse's neck and seeing the blood run off my elbow. Then the dragonflies came and that meant the beginning of the end for the mosquitoes. How I loved them and how beautiful I thought they were. I still think so."[84] Although Beldam does not underrate the irritation caused by mosquitoes, she focuses on the attendant beauty, thus underlining the point that making life more pleasant in the valley meant accommodation to the mosquito, not necessarily extermination of habitat.

Mosquito imagery, however, is suffused with the violence of war. *Qwál*, meaning mosquito, is the name of a warrior from the Sumas Band who was famous for his quick "in and out" style of attack.[85] Extensive studies on mosquitoes, especially concerning disease vectors and control through pesticides such as DDT,[86] were carried out during the Second World War, and a renowned fighter aircraft was named the Mosquito. Storytellers searching for historical causality often connect the political will to complete the Sumas reclamation with the outbreak of the First World War, the demand for agricultural products, and, later, the need of arable land for soldier settlement.[87] Oddly enough, even the official protectors of migratory wildlife were strong advocates of wetlands drainage in the Lower Fraser Valley. When framed in wartime rhetoric, this irony becomes less curious. The campaign to drain the lake was aided considerably not only by the war waged in Europe but by the civil war against the mosquito. The operative word, resonating beyond the insect world, was "control."

From 1887 until 1898, as a result of the hunting and recording skills of Canada's esteemed naturalist-artist, Major Allan Brooks, the region of Sumas Lake was "more thoroughly worked ornithologically than any other portion of the Province."[88] Brooks, "eighteen and chuck full of enthusiasm," first came to the area in May 1887 with his father, W.E. Brooks, who had bought a farm close to the village of Chilliwack. Like other naturalists of his generation who focused more on structure than

Sharp-shinned hawk, Sumas, painted by Allan Brooks, 1905
(Laing, *Allan Brooks*, 70, photograph courtesy of
the Royal British Columbia Museum)

behaviour, Brooks killed to know, and he shot and trapped many of his listed 253 species of birds in the area, as well as 60 species of mammals.[89] In the late fall of 1894 he noted a dozen large flocks of whistling swans on Sumas Lake, and he recorded many changes during these years and thereafter, especially as a result of harrassment and overhunting. Brooks himself was a market hunter for museums in Europe and North America. His Sumas Lake specimens of sandpipers in Berkeley Museum of Vertebrate Zoology (pectoral sandpiper, Baird's sandpiper, least sandpiper, and western sandpiper), all now vanished from the Sumas area, are in groups of threes and fours, several females containing eggs, shot mainly in late summer and early fall.[90] In 1917 he wrote that many species, such as Hutchin's goose (Taverner's Canada goose), "mostly pass over now, as they are too much disturbed."[91]

The lake, full of Dolly Varden trout, salmon, and sturgeon, continued to provide the locals with "happy and profitable hunting grounds."[92] But the fish were a prized and contested resource. Terry Glavin recently called sturgeon "living dinosaurs that emerged in the Upper Cretaceous period of the Mesozoic era 98 million years ago and have remained unchanged for the past two million years."[93] But he also noted that Indian Superintendent Vowell had declared in 1905 that these fish, known to grow more than twelve feet in length, were practically extinct as a result of commercial overfishing. In April 1905 the fisheries department seized the nets of Indians fishing for sturgeon in Sumas Lake, apparently because the nets were blocking the passage of salmon to the spawning grounds. The *Chilliwack Progress* noted that "from the standpoint of the side of the Indians it is nothing short of a calamity, as at this season of the year their only livelihood has been taken away, and they are consequently in a state of destitution."[94]

A concern with regulations and wildlife conservation in Canada originated – on a federal level – with civil servants rather than elected officials and not until very late in the nineteenth century. Janet Foster, a scholar of Canadian conservation, has blamed this belated interest on "an uninhabited frontier, the myth of superabundance, an era of exploitation and lack of knowledge about wildlife, the political climate of the National Policy and the division of powers under the British North America Act."[95] Questioning several areas of Foster's "uninhabited frontier," I would add that British Columbians who devalued the local land and waterscape, and those who first lived there, also encouraged disinterest in local habitat conservation.

Part of the Brooks bird collection, *ca* 1930 (Laing, *Allan Brooks*, 160, photograph courtesy of the Royal British Columbia Museum)

Sturgeon fishing. Stó:lō fishermen with Fraser River catch; (*left to right*) Alfred Cline, Joe Louie, and Ed Louie, date unknown (Chilliwack Archives, P-656)

Protection of land by the federal government meant strict control and a high degree of management. Divided into seven small parcels of seasonally dry land, the Sumas Indian reserves were vulnerable to further reductions. As early as 1903, a Sumas reserve southwest of the lake was considered for surrender to a farmer in Abbotsford. The Indian superintendent asked the local Indian agent to look into the matter, and he reported, "It is true they are not making a great deal of use of their ground (one old man plants potatoes there each year), but we expect better from the younger generation growing up ... I have not called the Indians together to discuss the surrender of this Reserve as knowing their sentiments on this matter I know it would be useless."[96] A lingering irritant to the Sumas newcomers, the issue of sale, was again raised during the McKenna-McBride commission. Although lands were reduced from the Upper Sumas Reserve (no. 6, Kilgard),[97] this particular reserve (no. 7) was not sold at this time either. However, the notorious Duncan Campbell Scott, deputy superintendent general of Indian affairs, persisted, pressuring the sale with the cause of "Returned Soldier Settlement," and he succeeded in obtaining a surrender on Hallowe'en 1919.[98]

The extension of the net of control over land, fish, fowl, and mosquitoes required a specialist, a manager – a new breed of person altogether. The dominion entomologist Gordon Hewitt was the most energetic and influential of the officials interested in conservation. Hewitt secured the momentous Treaty for International Protection of Migratory Birds, signed with the United States in 1916. The federal government thus was empowered to make rules enhancing the protection of migratory birds, establishing closed seasons, issuing hunting permits, and designating endangered species.

Sumas Lake, which was mainly used by wildfowl as a stopping place or wintering area on flights to and from their Arctic breeding grounds,[99] was a prime candidate for regulation. Unfortunately, these geese, ducks, and swans who needed undisturbed habitat for feeding, loafing, and preening were aided very little by the treaty. Although it ignored Aboriginal rights to hunt, British Columbia representatives were intransigent on their frontier rights to hunt wherever, whenever, and whatever they wanted. Hewitt negotiated major concessions for the province which became major concessions for the market hunters at Sumas Lake. Wildfowl could be shot by sportsmen with permits after 31 March "if injurious to agriculture" (which Hewitt admitted was an unlikely occurrence); the five-year closed season on wood duck was rescinded, and British Columbia was specially exempted from a ten-year closed season on cranes, swans, and curlews.[100]

Vancouver's small armies of weekend hunters, who had used the B.C. Electric Railway since its completion in the fall of 1910, continued to stop off at the Sumas Lake shooting range until the lake was divided into private fields, in which soon even the grazing geese were diminished by good aim and gunshot. It was the B.C. Electric Railway, rather than the new regulations, that "brought the first radical change" to what sportswoman Beldam called her "security" and "privileged isolation." Hewitt also revised the Northwest Game Act,[101] sat on the interdepartmental Wild Life Protection Advisory Board with Scott,[102] and transformed the Dominion Entomological Service into a major branch of the Department of Agriculture, with twelve laboratories spread across Canada. He even managed to squeeze in a visit to the Lower Fraser Valley to address the burgeoning mosquito issue.

A change in government in 1916 at the provincial level prioritized "progressive" agricultural strategies and land settlement. Before the war's end, Premier "Honest" John Oliver, a farmer from Delta, encouraged drainage of the lake as part of his plans for the employment and re-establishment of returning soldiers.[103] His minister of agriculture, the farmer-politician from Chilliwack, "Honest Abe" E.D. Barrow, would later consider the Sumas Reclamation Project his finest political achievement.[104] In 1917 the locally elected dyke commissioners were deposed, and the government's Land Settlement Board assumed their debts and responsibilities. The cost of the dyking and drainage was to be shared between the sale of the lake bottom lands and taxation of the local farmers. Thus, any proposed scheme required the cooperation of the dominion government as well as the Sumas landowners. According to the *Abbotsford Post*, the advisory board meeting in July 1918 concluded that "the district did not want a political dyke, it wanted a scientific dyke, and it was generally conceded that unanimity was the essential factor in success and that discussions on engineering schemes led to nothing."[105]

Barrow needed to sustain the project's momentum, and what had been a particularly intense mosquito season in July 1918 provided both a political and a scientific opportunity. As the female mosquitoes searched for the protein blood meals that would mature their eggs, the newspapers lamented and laid blame. One article in favour of drainage argued that "had it not been for the mosquito pest, the Fraser Valley would have had hundreds more settlers."[106] That September, Barrow organized the first conference ever held specifically to discuss the mosquito. The newspapers – with headlines declaring that the "Mighty Mosquito Must Migrate" to the "wilds of Potsdam" – exuded the battle rhetoric of wartime and quoted Barrow's honouring of local women who, acting as courageously as the women of Great Britain, had "stuck to their fruitpicking despite the fierce offensive of the mosquito."[107]

At the conference, Barrow declared, "To further delay action looking towards the eradication of the mosquito pest in the Fraser Valley, is nothing short of criminal neglect." There followed a speech by Hewitt, which was quoted extensively in the local newspaper; it supported the experiential knowledge of the popular farmer Barrow with the rhetoric of specialist scientific authority. Hewitt advised, "The best policy would be to obtain a small commission, covering the whole mosquito area, but lifted out of local interests and party politics. An independent body should be responsible for this work getting the advice from an expert. This would give authority of action." The fewer locals involved in giving orders, the greater would be the extent of the mobilization.

Among those assembled at the conference was the dairy farmer Sam Smith, "whose cows eat the grass even if the oil was on it and he thought it did them good." Hewitt informed the crowd that oil was "not a cure-all. Reclamation and drainage were the only true remedies for the mosquito." Hewitt's chief assistant in British Columbia, who until 1917 had been in charge of the Entomological Laboratory at the dominion's Agassiz Experimental Farm, urged full cooperation. A year earlier he had also advised biological control measures, including stocking permanent bodies of water with small fish to keep the mosquito population in check.[108]

On 20 October 1917 the fish of Sumas Lake were identified as important creatures in themselves by the head bureaucrat in the federal department responsible for fisheries, who explained, "As this lake, together with Sumas river, Vedder river and Cultus lake, – all of which it is understood would be affected, – form an extensive and valuable spawning area for the different species of salmon, it is important to know, before such work is undertaken, whether it would be detrimental to the fisheries."[109] The Department of the Interior replied:

With the diversion of the Vedder directly into the Fraser, the spawning grounds on this stream should not be interfered with, as the salmon would be able to swim up the new channel and spawn in the upper reaches of the river. Cultus lake, to which you refer in your letter, would not be affected by the scheme. Sumas lake, however, would be entirely drained and the lands forming the bed and shores thereof transformed into most valuable agricultural land. With the intimate knowledge of the Province of B.C. which you possess, you will readily realize the value of a level tract, comprising approximately 30,000 acres, possessing soil as fertile as any in the Province, and which is situated practically at the door of two of our largest coast cities ... It is necessary to appreciate the tremendous value of this area and effect the agricultural development of the same will have on this whole district, when considering the case.[110]

Subsequently, save for a telegram from the chief inspector of fisheries to the Land Settlement Board in 1922 asking "when action may be expected to permit ascent spawning salmon to Sumas Lake," fish did not appear as a major topic of drainage considerations.[111]

The political discussion was not about keeping expansive bodies of water for natural mosquito control and not about maintaining wildlife, fishing places and hunting grounds; it was about reclaiming and controlling land for agriculture and about mosquito extermination. If Gordon Hewitt, touted as Canada's Father of Conservation, had taken the time to gaze out onto the wetlands surrounding the lake, what would he have seen? Perhaps he saw a foregone conclusion: the indigenous willow, rose, cranberry bushes, and crabapple were increasingly being cleared away, and the overhunted dominion grasslands dedicated to pasture were not ideal habitat for wildfowl. Two years earlier, the hunter-naturalist Brooks had written of the Chilliwack-Sumas area: "Most of the marshes have been drained so the region will never accommodate breeding waterfowl to any extent."[112] But if Hewitt, the man supposedly most sensitive to the need for wildlands and bird habitat, had been struck with mosquito myopia, who would represent Sumas Lake?

That year the dominion government extended more than a helping hand in the provincial government's propaganda effort to drain Sumas Lake. United against the mosquito, the scientific and strategic resources of dominion and province joined forces in a postwar geopolitical campaign that helped eliminate Sumas Lake efficiently, profitably, and finally. The control of the water and land under the auspices of the "mosquito pest" became an extension of the war effort. In 1919 the National Research Council, in cooperation with the dominion Department of Agriculture, sponsored an investigation of the Lower Fraser Valley mosquito population. The study continued to 1921, when the Canadian Air Board and the Department of Agriculture sent aircraft to conduct one of the first aerial entomological surveys in Canada's history. The completed report of Eric Hearle, assistant entomologist in charge of mosquito investigations for the dominion Department of Agriculture, became grist for his Master of Science degree, as well as the basis for the eradication of the mosquito through the draining of their breeding places throughout the Fraser Valley.

Hearle centred his campaign not at Sumas but at Mission, the area of the worst mosquito problem. He flew over Sumas Lake, and the local paper reported that, on landing, he announced that "the draining of a mile of the lake shore would result in the elimination of the greatest mosquito breeding ground in the Lower Mainland."[113] Hearle advanced the education of the public with exhibits, lectures, and magazine and newspaper articles, explaining, "Until recently, very few people in the affected area had any idea that mosquitoes were controllable, and the pest was suffered as a necessary evil. Like the tide and the weather it was considered to be unaffected by human intervention."[114] Dr H.G. Dyar of the Washington National Museum, one of the world's leading experts on mosquitoes, came to visit Hearle in mid-July 1920 and, as a newspaper article reported, collected many specimens and reinforced Hearle's recommendation that the only way to get rid of the pest was through dyking and pumping. At this time, Hearle made what he felt to be an important discovery – a new species of mosquito in the Fraser Canyon. He named it *hewitti*, probably after Gordon Hewitt who died at the age of thirty-six in 1920.[115]

Curiously, in Hearle's tabulation of information since 1910, mosquitoes proved to be troublesome only during 50 per cent of the summers.[116] Hearle's report admittedly paid only incidental attention to the natural predators of the mosquito. Nevertheless, he noted that considerable numbers were eaten by other insects in permanent bodies of water; controlled tests showed that one dragonfly could consume 195 mosquito larvae in nineteen hours. He recorded that the fry of trout and other fish were observed "on several occasions destroying great numbers of mosquito larvae. Large shoals of fry were sometimes seen following each other in constant succession around the edges of flood water, wherever it was fairly deep and free from much vegetation."[117] Shore birds at Sumas Lake also were observed destroying great numbers of mosquitoes. Although no examinations of stomach contents were made, Hearle noted that in New Jersey the stomach contents of one species of shore bird was found

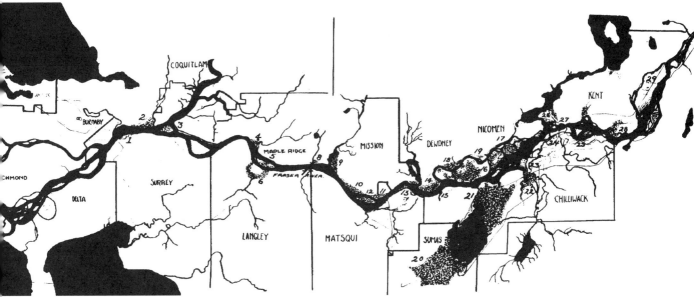

Map 5   Lower Fraser Valley, showing main floodwater breeding areas at
21-foot river level, compiled from aerial photographs and observations, 1921
Source: Hearle, *Mosquitoes of the Lower Fraser Valley*, 68

to consist of 53 per cent mosquito larvae. He also briefly mentioned bats and sala-
manders, and a recent damaging infection of parasitic worms in *Aedes vexans*; but,
again, few tests were made and no follow-up was suggested.

Hearle's final report was on the mosquito, not on an ecosystem,[118] and the remedy
– drainage – had already caused the lake to disappear by the time the report was
published in 1926. Specializing, zeroing in on the topic, he exterminated as many
needless words as possible and ignored the whole. The major work of dyking and
dredging was completed by the fall of 1923. When thoughts about a flood lake are
reduced to one of its tiniest and most irritating members, answers are straightforward. Hearle's conclusion was to guide dyking and drainage policy for the next
several years.[119] The Sumas Lake sphere of alternatives was drained, in part, by the
farmer-politician's experience and the expertise of entomological science, a combina-
tion producing powerful suasory discourse.

For the engineers and the drainage supporters who in the winter of 1919 voted
144–21 in favour of the Frank Sinclair plan (the plan that would finally drain the
lake), Sumas Lake was simply part of a "great and intricate problem" that had found
its solution.[120] There is a bleak poignancy to the anxious letter of the director of the
Reclamation Service for the Department of the Interior complaining of the "difficulty
of accurately defining the marginal lands" that were under federal control and were
due to be transferred to the province after drainage. Written during a blizzard on
15 February 1923, the letter repeated the advice that "the bed of Sumas Lake has
never been subdivided and if required this work could not be done until the water
has been drained away."[121] What became clear was not the definition of the "useless" marginal land, but the uselessness of this mission of cartographic translation.

Although hidden by eighteen inches of snow, the lake was indeed disappearing.
Twenty-seven acres of the forty-nine-acre Aylechootlook reserve (Sumas Reserve no. 5)
had been "wiped out" by a dyke that had been constructed by the authority of the
Land Settlement Board to divert and contain the Vedder River – an integral part of the
lake drainage project. In this instance of land reduction, permission was not even re-
quested. The chairman of the board admitted to the chief inspector of Indian agencies
that the board had failed to make an application for the land as it had been
instructed to do, but he felt that he owed nothing to the Indians whose remaining
twenty-two acres obviously were improved by construction of the dyke.[122]

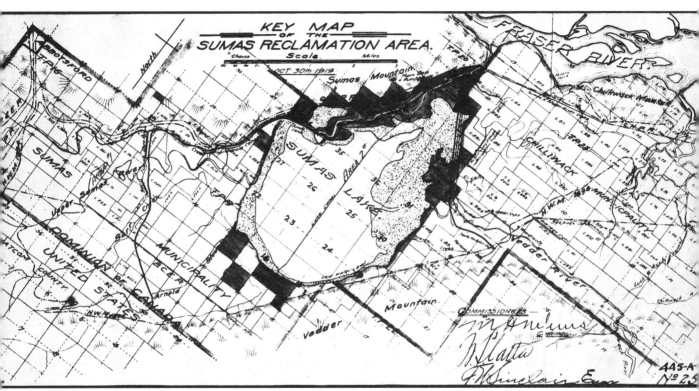

Map 6   Key map of the Sumas Reclamation Area, October 1919
Source: NA, RG89/269/3594

After almost a full year of pumping with the largest pump facility in the Dominion of Canada, the last waters of Sumas Lake were drained into the Fraser River in June 1924. The Cultus Lake Park Committee was formed, and in May it was tendering boat and ice-cream concessions in its bid to promote and manage the nearest existing lake as a public park.[123] Beldam writes that after the drainage, "the peaceful, leisurely times were gone."[124] She was twenty at the time; the passing of idealized notions of innocence and childhood was perhaps linked to the loss of the lake. But lamenting a purity and authenticity that was overrun, disappeared, is problematic. The hybrid place became another. Slowed by the first crop of willow trees, the lake land was bought up by individual and company interests, and the sandy soil eventually began to nurture clover, hops, and tobacco. The wild sweet potato that grew beside the lake could no longer be harvested by Stó:lō families; but First Nations people from up and down the valley would gather yearly to harvest the hops on the lake bottom.[125]

Stories are told of giant sturgeon that remained in the marshy areas of the fields, met by the plough rather than the returning waters of the lake. A local farmer reported that flocks of ducks maintained their landing patterns onto the "lake" for many years. Now, more than seventy years after the "reclamation project," small fish get stuck in the drainpipes, salmon are found in the drainage ditches, and sturgeon are sighted swimming back and forth in front of the pumphouse. They move along ancient routes to homewaters, caught in mechanisms of creation and eradication.

Sumas Lake, seen from the B.C. Electric substation on Vedder Mountain, *ca* 1916
(MSA Museum Archives, P-5005)

Sumas Prairie, also from the substation, *ca* 1926 (MSA Museum Archives, P-4998)

Memory Device

The landscape and the waterscape – what my mother calls our homescape[1] – is full of stories. Sometimes encountering these stories is simply a pleasant matter of walking outdoors with a knowledgeable elder. Sometimes, because not all narrative traditions are passed down and people die, and because the land and water have been altered so much that the story may be lost, our access to homescape history is restricted. Today, if you were to drive east between the rapidly growing cities of Abbotsford and Chilliwack, you would have little sense that your car was travelling over land that was once covered by water, past lakefront beaches and ridges that for a few decades bore such names as York, Bowman, and Michaud. A government "stop of interest" plaque beside the road describes the benefits of the reclamation project and thus reflects the general thrust of official history. You would know Sumas Lake only as water thankfully gone unless you were fortunate enough to learn a few good stories that would help you care about where you are and what was there.

Sumas Lake images are forms of restricted access to the lake. Yet they play an important role in reminding us of life in the community before drainage. When visiting the homes of men and women who remembered the lake, I was struck by the presence of Sumas Lake photographs and paintings. Mrs M led me down her hallway and pointed to a framed photograph. "There it is," she said, "that lake."[2] And by its shore she sat, gazing at a camera almost three-quarters of a century ago. Later, she

SUMAS LAKE RECLAMATION

In 1924, by a system of stream diversions, dams, dykes, canals and pumps, 33,000 acres of fertile land were reclaimed from Sumas Lake. Few areas in B.C. have such rich soil with transportation and markets in close proximity. Produce of the mixed farming on this deep lake-bottom land is an important factor in the economy of our mountainous province.

PROVINCE OF
BRITISH COLUMBIA
19 67

Stop of interest, Trans-Canada Highway
(photo by John B. Cameron, August 1994)

showed me a picture of Sumas Lake, composed in warm blues and yellows, painted by Louie Alexander, a young woman from Winnipeg who used to visit every summer and allowed Mrs M to watch her work if she was quiet.

Mr G was reluctant to be pegged as a lake lover. "It was just a lake,"[3] he said, perhaps reminding me that my subjectivity was becoming too apparent. His living room deeply impressed me; not only did his picture windows offer a view of the lake bottom lands, but a large painting of Sumas Lake, in golds and greens, had the privileged place in the room. Yes, it matched the furniture. But which came first, the painting or the couch, I failed to ask. Mr G had painted it years after the drainage, working from a photograph and visiting the spot where the picture had been taken.

At home, Mr G modestly denounced his own talent and memory. But later, as he drove me around the lake bottom, he displayed great knowledge of absent landmarks: community halls, roads, altered ridges. He said he often drove the route on his own – though it was "just a lake." Mr G's memory tour formed a clear pattern in an admittedly small sample of interviewees: when those who remembered the lake accompanied me to the place where the lake used to be, when they gestured to familiar yet altered sites, memory and story flowed.

Mrs M pointed out a remnant of the old Yale Road that used to take her to her grandparents' home by the lake. She asked, "Can you just see yourself in a horse and buggy trotting along here?" Beside her, I could. "There's the cliff where the waves used to splash up." Mr H was quick to say he had little to offer me because he was so young when the lake was drained. But then he gestured across the road at the Kilgard reserve. At the site where his brother had drowned in Sumas Lake, he had constructed and encouraged a small pond.[5] As men and women invested paintings, photographs, and drained landscape with story, they offered not only new content for history but new eyes, new ears.

The American environmental historian William Cronon recently stated that stories are our "chief moral compass in the world."[6] To extend his metaphor a little, stories help orient us with respect to our lives and, in no small measure, with respect to the places in which we live. Our storytellers invest places with meaning, and, reflexively, these places orient the stories they tell. In the context of the debate regarding the value of oral tradition for historical research, such a provocative idea gives rise to many questions. One of the most challenging is posed by Julie Cruikshank when she

Mr G at home, looking towards Sumas Prairie (photo by L. Cameron, March 1994)

Painting of Sumas Lake by Mr G (photo by L. Cameron, March 1994)

Louie Alexander painting beside Sumas Lake (NSC, *ASM News*)

Painting of Sumas Lake by Louie Alexander, owned by Mrs M
(photo by L. Cameron, March 1994)

says, "All societies have characteristic narrative structures that help members construct and maintain knowledge of the world."[7] If historians affirm this view from anthropology – and I think they should – can the stories about the same place told by people with potentially very different narrative structures be effectively compared? And what happens to stories, these moral compasses, when places change?

In order to diversify ways of knowing Sumas Lake, I have chosen to focus on stories that were told to me indirectly. They all come from the 1950s and early 1960s when I was not alive and when Sumas Lake had been dead for thirty years. Some were written into history books; some were told to another person who taped or transcribed them. These latter stories were told by men and women who composed in an indigenous narrative tradition, a tradition of storytelling that first made this lake meaningful to people. Stó:lō oral tradition thrives in certain places. But one reason for my analysis of the archive rather than my own fieldwork is perhaps best summed up by a woman who said to me, "I went to school before the lake was drained and when I came back, it was gone."[8] I was trying to learn stories about the rupture of community through lake drainage, but I was made to understand that being sent away from home to a residential school was an experience that often removed the opportunity to learn stories about home. There are political and methodological dangers in considering oral and written narrative in the same discussion, but I seek a place of warmth, a gathering together, in the midst of shifting and disputed intellectual territory.

The question "How deep, how big was Sumas Lake?" is not irrelevant, but here I want to stress that each measurement of the lake comes with its own story. Note that the lake is measured in acreage (a unit of measurement relating to land) and that the drainage project is termed a "reclamation" of land, not a "draining of water." Water is something superfluous, something floating on top. To reclaim something is to assume you somehow lost it. Can one lose a lake bottom? But a reclamation is also a redemption – a turning from sinful ways. To reclaim is also to bring something like a desert or a marsh into a condition that can support crops or life. I am not interested here in making two separate piles of reliable versus nonreliable descriptions. I aim to learn from – not simply debunk – different ways of storytelling while asking, "What makes certain stories stick?"

A blatant and localized example of what I tend to worry about might be my experience of listening to the thirty-year-old reel-to-reel tapes of a Fraser Valley historian and radio broadcaster named Casey Wells. One tape made in the 1960s was an educational acousti-guide – an audio tour of valley history – using designated places to tell a story about the past. As Wells promised his student-listeners, "We will visit the actual places where many exciting and important events took place – where disasters occurred and where there were achievements by both native Indians and white pioneers. You will visit the exact locations; you will hear the authentic stories; and you can say, 'It happened here' "[9] – a statement that Wells always solemnized by striking a gong. But despite his clear voice and crisp directions, the experience of listening to these stories today, in our present landscape, is a disorienting one. Only thirty years later, many of Wells's designated places are gone or are significantly altered. The stories, though preserved on tape, have lost their moorings and the tour becomes semi-incoherent.

Now as the Fraser Valley continues to be one of the fastest-changing places within one of the most rapidly growing regions in Canada, similar Wellsian accounts of incoherency become commonplace. And the practising historian's job becomes more difficult, though as necessary as ever to the community to which she or he belongs. Sumas Lake historiography offers insight into how historians have made dramatic change understandable and perhaps survivable. An English naturalist on the International Boundary Commission dubbed Sumas Lake a "second Eden,"[10] romantic and beautiful beyond compare; a chief of the Sumas Band called it "one of the greatest spawning grounds there is";[11] a UBC geographer wrote of it as "the great impediment to east-west transportation through the Lower Mainland."[12] These descriptions are not merely right or wrong. For as we stand in the ironic position of knowing that Sumas Lake no longer exists, each phrase implies a different possible environmental history of the area, each articulating a particular origin and destiny.[13]

Written histories about Sumas Lake have two basic plot lines. Unilinear, these plot lines are extensions of the understanding that continuous narrative helps to lend coherence to life. Recent ecological histories and personal memoirs have the form of a downhill slope – a degression into a life that is less satisfying, less abundant, and less free. But by far the dominant plot line is that of increasing human progress; the reclamation of Sumas Lake serves to illustrate another step in civilization's growing control of the place it had come to inhabit. The story is one of the most compelling stories of the West: sturdy farmers turn undeveloped vastness into an abundant garden. In 1948 George White concluded his article on the "The Development of the Eastern Fraser Valley" with the following:

Looking over the whole reclamation project after a period of twenty years, one cannot but feel that it was well worth while and that it will repay all the time and money spent on it. For countless years there lay an 8,000 acre area of mud and water that was too shallow for navigation and probably too deep for the comfort of duck-hunters, who were the only ones to get even a few day's use of it. In addition, it was probably the finest breeding-ground in the whole Dominion of Canada for mosquitoes. Today there exists as fine a stretch of farming country as one could wish to see, with excellent soil, ample water-supply, a splendid system of drainage, and only 50 miles from an urban community that already contains nearly 400,000 people. It is difficult to conceive of any farm lands in North America more favorably situated.[14]

Repeating almost word for word the official report of the provincial Land Settlement Board that was in charge of the drainage project,[15] the phrase "probably the finest breeding ground for mosquitoes in the Dominion of Canada" continues to appear in Sumas Lake histories.[16] The beauty of the final pastoral image is underlined by White's assertion that the lake was worthless, deserving annihilation.

The lake was also joined to an opponent, and thus its drainage reinforces the magnitude of human accomplishment. Bruce Hutchison, in his 1950 book *The Fraser,* linked the taming of the formidable river, "forever mad, ravenous and lonely,"[17] with the drainage of Sumas Lake. The Fraser River, "the prodigal waste of energy," often flooded into the tidal lake during the spring freshets, and Hutchison lauded Ed Barrow, the politician/farmer who pushed for the lake's drainage, for realizing "the dream that has become one of British Columbia's proudest possessions." Even when it enters the gentle and open Fraser Valley, where "man now grows his crops and feeds his dairy herds" on its silt, "still the river is not to be trusted. It continually threatens and often overflows the dikes he has built against it."[18] Putting the Vedder River in a "straitjacket" and pumping out Sumas Lake was, in Hutchison's analysis, the greatest work in our mastery of the Fraser River. The madness was tamed – wrongs were righted – because of strong faith in a technological dream.

The words of older general histories weave into the most recent ones. Margaret Ormsby's highly influential *British Columbia: A History* (1958) very briefly recounts the reclamation of the "marshy lands of Sumas Prairie."[19] Similarly, in *The West beyond the West* (1991), Jean Barman chooses the word "marsh" over "lake" when she writes, "The Sumas reclamation project drained thirty thousand marshy acres of the fertile Lower Fraser Valley for mixed and dairy farming."[20] Sumas Lake is drained and framed in policy cause and effect within both the linear logic of print and the spatial expansion of a young province. And agricultural communities such as Yarrow that extend their roots onto the claimed lakebed are indebted to these scholarly stories and to the disappearance of the lake as they, in their local histories, write of their origins and destiny.

The success and coherence of these local histories is also indebted to the disappearance of First Peoples; cursory descriptions of static Native cultures are simply soaked up by the dramatic action of reclamation that follows. Named landscapes and waterscapes are recognized but absorbed. Obviously, my tone indicates derision for this whitewashing of history, but I must pause to point out that at one time most newcomers believed these stories, *lived by* these stories. That many still do is perhaps reason enough to analyse and deconstruct their "mythical" status, yet we are not obligated to deride the settlers' myth while we uphold the myth of others. By focusing on the lake in the same time period, we may – by listening to tapes and reading transcripts – begin to appreciate how the productions of oral and written knowlege are not unrelated – indeed how they help to illuminate each other.

Not all non-Native storytellers ignored Native voices and ideas. In part, these people reinforced the notion of peaceful Native-newcomer relations, removing any culpability of Native dispossession from the hands of honest and decent Christian folk. But despite the potentially uneven power dynamic, non-Native interest in Native history has qualified the garden myth with voices that did not belong to Adam or Eve. That particular story did not capture all imaginations perhaps because, as the historian Donald Worster suggests, it was "filled with all the unresolved contradictions of innocence."[21] The garden story optimistically affirmed the story of progress through economic development; nevertheless, the same story was a celebration of humanity's successful escape from "civilized" development.

Under the auspices of the investigative expertise of a modern and more advanced culture, ethnographers have been recording and transcribing indigenous stories of the Fraser Valley for several decades. Charles Hill-Tout declared in the 1890s that the areas around Sumas "seem to possess but few folk-tales, or else they have forgotten them."[22] But students of oral tradition and oral history in the 1950s and 1960s were more fortunate listeners. In the summer of 1950, Norman Lerman, an anthropology student from Western Washington University, listened to a large number of stories from Native people in the Nooksack-Sumas-Chilliwack region and analysed their plots and motifs. Oliver Wells, brother of Casey, was intent on discovering the location and meaning of place-names in the Fraser Valley and recorded many Native friends in the 1960s. CBC Radio's Imbert Orchard travelled around the Fraser Valley recording stories for a radio documentary in the early 1960s. All these stories exist as fragments, some written into books, some archived on cassette and reel-to-reel tapes, pulled from their fieldwork context to exist in the world of libraries and archives around the region.

To explore these stories by focusing on place – just as I explored the stories of White and Hutchison – is to risk misrepresentation and misuse once again. I am likely to underestimate the story's complexity. Further, the oral traditions that I have listened to on tape and read in books from the 1950s and 1960s are mediated by the ethnographer's documenting techniques and driven by the ethnographer's questions. Yet they have value beyond the mere fact that they exist. By attending to how these stories may help us contextualize and understand contemporary events, we may find an authentic opening to the historical knowledge of Sumas Lake.

As I listened to the voices and read the transcriptions aloud, I began to consider the physical significance of a proposition that seems to emerge from particular studies of oral culture.[23] While written narratives, like histories, tend to rely on time – the time-line of dates – to talk about events in space, oral traditions tend to employ the place-names of space to talk about events in time. Books contain stories, but in a world of lakes and mountains there are many other possibly durable visual loci that are capable of holding, reinforcing, and retaining stories. In Lerman's typescript, he gives some indication of how his informants used the land- and waterscapes around them to reinforce particular points of a story, to show how and where it happened.

For instance, as Gus Commodore told the story of Thunderbird, Lerman noted how Commodore "pointed to the hills above Kilgard"[24] (Sumas no. 6 reserve) to show where a young man had had a dream-vision in which he was told how to become Thunderbird. A 1993 field trip with Sonny McHalsie of the Stó:lō Tribal Council drove home to me the continuing importance of pointing, touching, and witnessing tangible landscape features in the present in order to ground oral tradition transmitted from the past. Thereby, story was and is attached to territory, and anyone listening can never again look at the hills in the same way. What I knew only as a strip of highway heading up the Trans-Canada to Hope became a named homescape full of story and strong relationships. One oral narrative tells of a great flood that occurred in the Fraser Valley and how the people saved themselves by climbing up Sumas Mountain, which they then called *Kw'ekw'e'iqw* (meaning "head sticking up out of the ground"). You can still see the caves where they stayed dry.[25] A local, perhaps, can point them out.

Not surprisingly, the place-name Sumas appears in many stories of the 1950s. All the storytellers were old enough to remember the lake and its drainage. In 1950 Mrs Agnes James, born at Matsqui, west of Sumas, in 1885, told Lerman the story of Mink. The scene is set at Sumas Lake and the mention of the toponym gives her the opportunity to explain that Sumas Prairie had recently been covered by a large lake.[26] Food gathering activity is described as Blue Crane digs for wild vegetables at the lake's edge.

Gus Commodore tells the Mosquito Story (similar to a plot used by coastal groups), placing it at a beach at Sumas Lake. In condensed form,[27] the story is as follows. The young people who go to the beach to swim fail to share the best parts of their lunch with their friend Humpy salmon. Humpy then hollers for the giant Saskts, who hears and comes with a basket to capture the children, including Humpy. The children manage to outwit the giant, who intends to eat them, and they shove him into his own fire. "When he was burning, the giant said, 'I won't be killing or eating anybody else.' The children said, 'We'll not destroy you altogether. We'll have something to remember you by.' The leader of the bigger boys said to the sparks that were going up, 'You'll be mosquitos …' He said to the bigger sparks, 'You'll be sandflies.' That's it."[28]

More commonly, there are stories of the lake bottom. Time is rarely specific in these stories; the speakers use terms such as "long ago." But place certainly is specific. Place also appears to be consistent across many accounts of dramatic events such as drought. The origin story of the drought was told by different storytellers to different interviewers in different places and at different times. Yet each storyteller linked the tale to the area where Sumas Lake used to be. In brief, the story begins with disaster, a famine, a drought in which all life dries up. Everyone dies except one man and one woman. The woman lives at the south end of the prairie near a creek or a puddle and is able to survive through her ingenuity and the few remnants of living things. The man and woman eventually find each other and together they repopulate the area and bring back life and language.

The variations in the stories are instructive and in part gendered. Mrs Harry Uslick, born in Sardis, east of Sumas Lake, was interviewed by Norman Lerman in 1950.[29] Her narration follows the activities of the woman who survives beside a creek. This woman's amazing innovations are able to save the starving man, who has found her by crawling over to the creek. The woman, after noticing some trout, "took her hairs, one at a time, and spliced them to make them longer. Then she took wild gooseberry thorn for her hook." Uslick's story is laden with "traditional" information relevant to Stó:lō women, including ways of making fire with "old time matches" and methods of drying and curing fish. Conversely, the male storytellers follow the male protagonist as he travels alone from territory to territory looking for people and finding nothing and no one. Joe Louie, interviewed by Imbert Orchard in 1967 in Everson, Washington, was a well-travelled man like the character in his story, who hiked from Nooksack in Washington State to the Sumas Band's Kilgard reserve before finding the woman from Cultus Lake down on Sumas Flat living off little red pinfish in the remaining puddles of water.[30]

The variations on this story by Dan Milo of Skowkale[31] and Amy Cooper of Soowhalie[32] were told in the 1960s. Each emphasized the post-drainage landscape context – places you can still go to. After the drought, any lake has, of course, disappeared; all that is left is creeks and puddles. The listener is given familiar place-names and a contemporary landscape context in which to situate the story: Kilgard, Yarrow, South Sumas. "They call it South Sumas now. There's a creek that runs from here over to South Sumas."[33] But the link between contemporary landscape and story became dramatically apparent as I listened to Joe Louie. Slowly I began to realize that he tied the drought story explicitly to the dry lake bottom, helping Imbert Orchard understand the story's geography:

You see, yeah … they brought life, you see, and all living to the Fraser River … It was at the lake that they first met … you see they come down there to gather food and so forth, down to the lake. There was a big lake down there, you know, where they're drained out there, they use to come down there and gather up their sturgeon and steelheads in the spring of the year. Before they drained that ... That's where they met ... you see deep holes in there, you see, that left some water in the bottom, you see. And that's where she was found, you know, by this man there.

Here Louie seemed to be using the origin story to discuss and contextualize the lake drainage. In turn, this drainage story of catastrophe, more familiar as history to Orchard perhaps because he had read about it somewhere, helps the listener locate the actual place of the origin story. Using space to talk about events in time, Louie reflected on human innovation, the value of water and the "life and living" that comes with it.

Places and stories can interact in both the written and the oral traditions of storytelling. To encourage a continuation of the story about different stories, I wish to emphasize some connections. First, places may have rhetorical and material importance for the stories we tell. The place of Sumas Lake as "impediment," "beach," or "breadbasket" is implanted with meaning through story. Landscapes or waterscapes for an oral culture contain clues to the location of stories, and these stories are shaped and reshaped by different people living in different circumstances. The connection between place and story is neither direct nor linear, but places can act as memory devices that allow the transmission and conservation of cultural knowledge.[34] When written stories are taken out in memory to the place they refer to – whenever we drive over the lake bottom on the Trans-Canada Highway – they also rely on the memory device of place. We simply look or point for emphasis at the lake bottom, and our story's "rhetorical landscape"[35] reminds us of ends, origins. We can say, "It happened here."

Understood this way, even the buildings of former residential schools can be seen as powerful memory devices. Coqualeetza, a cultural organization serving the Stó:lō, has retained the principal's house of the former Coqualeetza Residential School. As an artifact on the landscape, it is a reminder of the story of segregated education and of removal from home. Now a Stó:lō art and craft store, it was recently used for the storage of the community's archive and library, thereby also acting as a place that helps assess that story.

Secondly, stories about dramatically changed places act as adaptive techniques to help people make dynamic environments coherent. When places with physical significance are gone, the rhetorical force of the stories to which they were connected is weakened; one can no longer point. In reference to altered space, from the Trans-Canada to the Transvaal, such a comment would seem to have relevance in any indigenous community experiencing "development." History is archived in the waterscape and landscape. When place-names no longer refer to anything tangible, the storytellers who have learned to use names such as Sumas Lake will find fewer and fewer listeners who can appreciate the spatial anchors and thus the stories.

But storytellers belong to a dynamic and flexible tradition. Their stories help communities deal with change. Certainly, the drought story of Uslick and Louie and the reclamation story of White and Hutchison have many differences. One laments a terrible drought, while the other celebrates drainage. In one, the water – without explanation – disappears; in the other, the lake is made to disappear because of the actions of people. The drought is framed by a very long time dimension and a small area of space, whereas the reclamation is framed by a very short time dimension and the spatial expansion of a nation. But viewed at the site where it happens, the natural disaster and the technological marvel are aspects of the same "outside" force that continues to regulate the water and the land.

Perhaps surprisingly, both are stories of human progress. Beginning with imagery of an environment harsh to human life, both end with the affirmation of human ingenuity and expansion on or near the lake bottom land. There is survival. Such happy endings are always up for alteration when a space is contested, as the bite out of the environment begins to itch and the monster we are creating becomes visible. Local schools now attend to the local area, creating "lake" tours and reassessing history in the light of lake drainage. Legal histories are being written for Native land and water claims. As the Barrowtown station continues to pump the lakebed, experts lament the soil erosion and admit that the flood hazard cannot be eliminated. Frequent handlers of the soil are advised to wear gloves to prevent potential injury from toxins in the water and ground. Engaged storytellers have much to make coherent if the landscape is to continue to support our stories of progress.

McGregor Ridge, which would have been an island when Sumas Lake was in flood (photo by L. Cameron, February 1994)

Lakemount Marsh, a remaining part of Sumas Lake currently operated by a private hunting club (photo by L. Cameron, February 1994)

Thirdly and most importantly, stories about place can inspire our moral awareness. Our histories undoubtedly do many things. Yet to ask what stories are good for us is, in some significant measure, to ask what places are good for us. A good story might make us care about the places where we spend our time and help us realize that these places affect who we are and the stories – whose stories, which stories – that we are able to tell. Stories about places can help bring back "the life and the living," reawakening a sense of wonder and respect for our homescapes. Combined with story, even the bite of a mosquito can reconnect us to a sense of place and the challenge of sharing it.

One More Byte

Ever since Laura began this work on Sumas Lake, I have been her irritant, her muse. She exhibits little affection for mosquitoes though she fancies herself to be extremely desirable to us. On the coldest winter day, she has seen one hover slowly, as if in a trance, across her computer screen towards her exposed typing fingers. The task was challenging, but after initial resistance, we pursued and persuaded her to see the wisdom of Marston Bates's lifelong attempt "to look at the world from the mosquito point of view."[1] Bates was a scientist who did not shun anthropomorphism but identified the difficulties of avoiding it and even praised metaphoric language ascribing emotions to insects. "Angry bees" aided his understanding of necessarily mediated reality. In the 1940s he extended his humanity to write an exceptional book – one of the few mosquito studies that was not simply a manual for the extermination of my kind.[2] Bates and others[3] have identified me as *Aedes vexans* of the tribe Culicidae from the order Diptera. Although the mosquito's "pest" or "monster" persona through which I now speak has a universal dimension, please understand that my particular perspective on history is also just that – particular.

In order for you to hear a history about Sumas Lake, someone must represent it. I depict the place in word, but I also represent the lake in a slightly different sense. Elected by the popular demand of local storytellers, I frequently represent (in the sense of a political agent)[4] the interests of Sumas Lake and its right to have existed.

As people keep saying, "It was probably the finest breeding ground in the whole ..." You know how it goes. Perhaps it is time for a new election. I feel pretty close to death, so let me begin. By all means wave your arms about, increase the blood circulation, but save your questions. Interaction is a special interest of mine, and I always make time for my audience.

Water is a particularly good subject for reflection. James Joyce listed, among many other qualities, its "universality, its democratic equality and constancy to its nature in seeking its own level: its metamorphoses as vapour, mist, cloud, rain, sleet, snow, hail ... its ubiquity as constituting 90% of the human body: the noxiousness of its effluvia in lacustrine marshes, pestilential fens, faded flowerwater, stagnant pools in the waning moon."[5] You may have heard my story before. Indeed, I hope you have. It is hardly a departure from everything that has come before. That is a task for modernizers, and I leave it to them.[6] I am no limnologist – that is to say, no lake expert – but with *Aedes vexans* being one of the species most attracted to light, firesides, and desk lamps where storytellers gather, I am a great observer of historical documents. *Aedes vexans* has one of the widest ranges of all mosquitoes and has been found in the Palearctic, Nearctic, and Oriental regions, as well as in Fiji, Samoa, and New Caledonia.[7] One was trapped by an airplane in Louisiana airspace at five thousand feet.[8] As Bates seemed to suggest, with all these studies going on and all this data being created, how can the scientist say the mosquito is of no use to humans?

But let us stop talking about utility. People have become weary and wary of claims of redemption through the technological fix – of DDT to fight us – and now, after Nile valley agriculture has been deprived of the annual nutrient-rich flood silt, and after continued flooding in the Midwest of the United States, people question the use of dams to counter flood. Who is pleased that Canada has diverted and dammed more water than any other nation on earth?[9] Many people are aware of trouble in the environment because of technological intervention, but one of the biggest sleeper issues, one of the greatest problems of environmental degradation, is people's real human capacity to forget a disappeared environment. With few stable physical reminders – trees, lakes, and buildings connected to stories that keep them in consciousness – people forget things that once were so important to their lives. Perhaps a purpose of history is to make people miss what they haven't experienced and to help them understand where they are. Open to possibilities of transforming everyday life, stories about places that people care about need retelling and re-thinking.

Interaction is quite the buzzword among users of electronic media. But action on each other is not something that the interface between computer and human necessarily exemplifies best. That medium is a little too predictable, not necessarily injecting life into history but possibly reducing the little that is there while consuming so much energy in the debugging process. Alternatively, oral history – an interactive method of learning stories from people in the flesh – is full of surprises. One does not begin an oral history project with the idea that one's assumptions will remain unchanged. The power dynamic is not controlled completely by the interviewer. "What sort of insects do you rejoice in where you come from?" the Gnat inquired. "I don't *rejoice* in insects at all," Alice explained, "because I'm rather afraid of them – at least the large kinds. But I can tell you the names of some of them."[10] Good questions shape answers, but Alice need not satisfy the Gnat's agenda.

The archive, that place containing, among other important documents, a naturalist's journal that acts as a mausoleum for my squashed relations, might be a lively and creative arena of debate. Here, in bits and pieces, lie stories in their seasons: the eggs, pupae, wrigglers, and final flight of an event, ideas emerging in the interface between past and present, document and rhetoric. But outside (wherever that begins for you), touching the ancient and what you hold as sacred, is where the wonderful interactive history occurs. And that is where I pose my challenge to history. How far are historians willing to go to honour time by honouring place? When does cultural/natural appreciation become appropriation? Where will they break the divide between the human and the non-human? What discomfort are they willing to accept, where are their flood limits? Electronics may connect us to an overflowing reservoir of information, but I suggest that my bite is, among other things, a big reminder that you are part of a greater network of relationships beyond those of your people-centred communites. And so I ask, How many bites of memory does the historian require?

Dear Ida

"When *your* are out camping
And with mosquitoes
are stamping
That is the time to
think of me.

Upper
Sumas } Your cosin Clytie
May 27th 1897.

Autograph of Clytie (Bowman) Greeno in Ida (Bowman) Campbell's
autograph book (NSC)

Notes

ABBREVIATIONS

BCARS British Columbia Archives and Record Services
CA Coqualeetza Archives
CHA Chilliwack Archives
CVA City of Vancouver Archives
MSA Matsqui-Sumas-Abbotsford Museum Society Archives
NA National Archives of Canada
NSC Neil Smith Collection
RDFCA Regional District of Fraser Cheam Archive
SBC Sumas Band Collection
STCC Stó:lō Tribal Council Collection
UBCSPE UBC Special Collections

OPENING

1 *Random House Webster's College Dictionary.*
2 Oliver Wells, *The Chilliwacks and Their Neighbours*, 219. A. McHalsie, cultural adviser, Stó:lō Nation, suggests that it derives from *sémath*, describing the thick reeds that grew there.

3 In terms of monetary value only: a 1993 Abbotsford District report states that Sumas Prairie has "an estimated agricultural invested value of some two hundred fifty million dollars. Return on investment per annum is around fifty million dollars Canadian" (Wright, *Barrowtown Pump Station*, 34).

4 Ibid.

5 His phrase resonates with the title of David Lowenthal's book, *The Past Is a Foreign Country*, which was taken from the first line of L.P. Hartley's novel *The Go-Between* (London: Hamish Hamilton, 1953): "The past is a foreign country, they do things differently there" (xvi).

6 Fraser, *Letters and Journals, 1806–1808*, 102.

7 Cited in Kroker, *Technology and the Canadian Mind*, 94.

8 Latour, *We Have Never Been Modern*, 104.

9 Ibid., 6.

10 Brand, *The Media Lab*, 7. Here I add "self-."

11 Landow, *Hypertext*, 4.

12 Cronon, Miles, and Gitlin, "Becoming West: Toward a New Meaning for Western History," in *Under an Open Sky*, 9.

13 In the hungry eyes of Canada's colonial government (Euro-Americans are Xwelítem, literally "hungry people," in the Stó:lō language of Halq'eméylem), "unoccupied land" was any land that did not have dwellings, settlements, cultivated areas, or graveyards. However, the definition has not been embraced by First Nations people. Under the Indian Act (1876, amended thereafter), tribal groups were not recognized. Rather, "Indian band" was chosen as the social/political unit, to be controlled by a local "Indian agency" and for which the Department of Indian Affairs would set aside lands called "Indian reserves."

14 Allan Smith, "The Writing of British Columbia History," 90, ftn.

15 Barry Peterson, "A Sense of Unoccupied Timelessness," *Weekend Sun*, 22 January 1994.

16 "Reasons for Judgement of the Honourable Chief Justice Alan McEachern," Supreme Court of British Columbia, no. 0843, Smithers Registry, 8 March 1991, 12.

17 Unit exam on Canadian history, Chilliwack Junior High School, age fifteen.

18 New Western History builds on the thoughts of many critics of Frederick Jackson Turner's frontier thesis that an area of free land and its constant recession through settlement explain American development and the American character. See, for instance, the work of Patricia Nelson Limerick, William Cronon, Donald Worster, and Richard White. Examples of Canadian histories that question the idea of free land/water and the image of settlers dwell-

ing in harmony with new possessions include Fisher and Coates, *Out of the Background*, and Newell's study of the indigenous B.C. fishery in her *Tangled Webs of History*.

19 For reflections on the interplay between myth and history, see Richard White, *It's Your Misfortune and None of My Own*, 613–31.

20 Deutsch, "Landscape of Enclaves," in Cronon, Miles, and Gitlin, *Under an Open Sky,* 131.

21 Landow, *Hypertext,* 2.

22 Ibid., 4.

23 The HyperCard prototype, for instance, was created in 1985.

24 Cronon, Miles, and Gitlin, "Becoming West," *Under an Open Sky,* 10.

25 Personal conference notes on George Landow's "Hyperliterature, Criticism and the Academy" (Beyond Gutenberg: Hypertext and the Future of the Humanities Conference, Yale University, 13 May 1994). At this conference, Landow reflected on his impatience with sound files, preferring "more bang for his buck."

26 With nearly 10 million users, this superhighway of information is an ever-expanding network that uses telecommunication lines to send large amounts of data between "sites" around the world. See Rheingold, *The Virtual Community*, 8.

27 Slotkin, *The Fatal Environment*, 45.

28 Fung, "Working through Cultural Appropriation," 16–24.

29 Landow, *Hypertext,* 185.

30 Personal conference notes on Edward Tufte's inaugural address, "Cognitive Arts" (Beyond Gutenberg Conference, Yale University, 13 May 1994).

31 Meyrowitz, *No Sense of Place*, 125.

32 Postman, *Technopoly*, 20.

33 Carr, *Time, Narrative and History*, 169.

34 Mumford, *The Myth of the Machine*, 106.

35 Personal conference notes on Michael Joyce's "(Re)Placing the Author: A Book in the Ruins" (Beyond Gutenberg Conference, Yale University, 13 May 1994).

36 Cited in the preface of *Hornby Island Official Community Plan*.

37 Hayden White, *Tropics of Discourse*, 91.

38 Fawcett, *Cambodia*, 58.

39 "Sir Douglas," 23 May 1994.

40 First Nations people whose displacement often provided this "room to expand" may be finding somewhat different reasons to join. For example, the potential of electronic hyper-

media to represent sensitively both oral and written knowledge is being explored by employees of Stó:lō Nation Canada.

41 Suttles, "Space and Time, Wind and Tide," 68.
42 See Williams, *The Country and the City*, for an important consideration of pastoral structure, the rural/urban division that also splits into past and future and the "problem of perspective."
43 See McClintock, *Imperial Leather: Race, Gender and Sexuality in the Colonial Contest*, 40."
44 Braudel, *The Mediterranean and the Mediterranean World in the Age of Phillip II*, 2:20–1. Structure, the geographic time of Braudel's *longue durée*, is likened to the sea depths. Conjuncture, the rhythms of "groups and groupings," is rendered as "swelling currents." Events of individual, short-term significance are surface waves, "crests of foam that the tides of history carry on their strong backs."
45 Hayden White, "Foucault Decoded," 28.
46 Buttimer, "Nature, Water Symbols and the Human Quest for Wholeness," 277.
47 Burgis and Morris, *The Natural History of Lakes*, 208.
48 Rheingold, *The Virtual Community*, 300.
49 Frye, in *Literary History of Canada*, ed. Klinck, 826.
50 Simmons, *Environmental History*, 185.

CHAPTER ONE

1 Massey, "A Place Called Home?" 164. Although Massey here is referring to the United Kingdom, I think her definition makes sense when thinking about "places" in British Columbia. In his *Keywords: A Vocabulary of Society and Nature*, Raymond Williams states that *place* is one of the most complex words in the English language. Anthropologist Wayne Suttles problematized a simple equation of place and community in the 1960s when he suggested that Coast Salish ideas of community may be based more on kin and intervillage ties than on the place of the village or reserve (Suttles, *Coast Salish Essays*, 209–20).
2 McClintock, *Imperial Leather*, 310.
3 Bloch, *The Historian's Craft*, 12.
4 See, for instance, Parr, *The Gender of Breadwinners*.
5 Rosaldo, "Doing Oral History," 89.
6 See, for instance, Gluck and Patai, *Women's Words*, and Thompson, *The Voice of the Past*.

7 Miles, "To Hear an Old Voice," in Cronon, Miles, and Gitlin, *Under an Open Sky*, 55.

8 Orchard, *Floodland and Forest*, 18.

9 In 1967 Orchard heard a history of Sumas Lake told by Joe Louie, an elder featured in *Floodland and Forest* (B.C. Archives and Record Services [BCARS], Imbert Orchard, "Mr. Joe Louie" [4/1/67], cassettes 437–1 & 2, Sound and Moving Division), see chapter 3, "Memory Device."

10 Orchard, *Floodland and Forest*, 7.

11 Major J.S. Matthews, "Mrs. Thomas Fraser York, Huntingdon, B.C." (City of Vancouver Archives [CVA], Add. MSS 54, vol. 13, York, Thomas Fraser).

12 Oliver Wells, *The Chilliwacks and Their Neighbours*, 189.

13 Ed Kelly (Matsqui-Sumas-Abbotsford archives [MSA], AH97). This version of the tape transcription differs somewhat from the MSA transcript in that I removed indications of speech pauses after consulting with the speaker.

14 Mr T, interview at his home, 22 March 1994.

15 Mrs M, interview on the lake bottom, 22 March 1994.

16 Orchard, *Floodland and Forest*, 59.

17 Ibid., 21.

18 Snyder, *Practice of the Wild*, 30.

19 Charlie Power (Chilliwack Archives [CHA], Add. MSS 401); Fred Zink, in Orchard, *Floodland and Forest*, 24; Ed Kelly (MSA, AH97); and Mr T, interview at his home, 22 March 1994.

20 Orchard, *Floodland and Forest*, 21.

21 Charlie Power (CHA, Add. MSS 401).

22 Bowen, preface to *Boss Whistle*.

23 Thompson, *Voice of the Past*, 105. However, as Keith Carlson suggested to me, it is also important to remember instances when the dynamic was reversed, such as the 1878 meeting in which the Indian reserve commissioner Gilbert Malcolm Sproat alone confronted a group of Lower Fraser Valley chiefs, who were protesting that incoming settlers were claiming land that Native people required. For further interpretations of Sproat's activities in the Lower Fraser Valley, see chapter 2 "Margins and Mosquitoes."

24 B.C. Archives and Record Services (BCARS), GR929, box 48, file 8, "Sumas Dyke Evidence, Agricultural Committee, Mon, 7th December/1925," 152.

25 Hofmeyr, "Nterata/The Wire," 70–1.

26 BCARS, British Columbia, *Papers Connected with the Indian Land Question*, 43.

27 Harris, "The Lower Mainland, 1820–81," 67.

28 Bob Smith, "The Reclamation of the Sumas Lands," 3.

29 McFarland, "Indian Reserve Cut-Offs in British Columbia," 45.

30 Ibid., 78.

31 Nash, *Wilderness and the American Mind*, 43.

32 BCARS, Add. MSS 1056, British Columbia, *Royal Commission on Indian Affairs for the Province of B.C. 1913–1915* (Union of B.C. Indian Chiefs), 137.

33 Ibid., 163.

34 Ibid., 152.

35 Ibid., 157.

36 Ibid., 155.

37 Ibid., 163.

38 McFarland, "Indian Reserve Cut-Offs in British Columbia," 76–7.

39 BCARS, Canada, Commission on Indian Affairs in General, 1913–1915, "Testimony of Indian agent for Sumas Indians in response to questions of Commissioner McKenna on Tuesday February 8th, 1915," 570.

40 Newell, *Tangled Webs*, 113.

41 Conference *Minutes* between the Allied Indian Tribes of B.C. and Dr D. Scott, 7–11 August 1923, 47.

42 Ibid., 45.

43 Canada, *Special Joint Committee of the Senate and House of Commons Appointed to Inquire into the Claims of the Allied Indian Tribes of British Columbia ... in June 1926*, 66. Even Duncan Campbell Scott, the deputy superintendent general of Indian affairs, complained of the "lack of distinctness in the stenographic report" in his own statements.

44 Canada, *Special Joint Committee* 125–6.

45 Ibid., 126.

46 Ibid., 127.

47 Parr, *The Gender of Breadwinners*, 97.

48 "B.C. Indian Leader Slams Germans, Greenpeace," *Vancouver Sun*, 3 February 1994; Mr Y, interview at his home, 3 February 1994.

49 See Donna Haraway, "Universal Donors in a Vampire Culture," 321–66, and Richard White, "Are You an Environmentalist or Do You Work for a Living? Work and Nature," 171–85, in Cronon, *Uncommon Ground*.

CHAPTER TWO

1 UBC Special Collections (UBCSPE), Lord, *At Home in the Wilderness*, 279–80.
2 Beldam, "Sumas Prairie," 35.
3 Ibid., 36.
4 Pred, *Making Histories*, 7.
5 Keddie, in "The Archeology of Mosquito Victims," takes the round-fish for oolichan. Bob Joe, interviewed by Oliver Wells, suggests that the fish were *q'oxel*, small fish that "came in schools ... full of bones, small bones" (Oliver Wells, *The Chilliwacks and Their Neighbours*, 117).
6 Cited in Oliver Wells, *The Chilliwack and Their Neighbours*, 116–17, ftn. See also UBCSPE, Lord, *The Naturalist in Vancouver Island and B.C.*, 1:99.
7 Native tradition speaks of the Chilliwack River once flowing into Sumas Lake before a log-jam diverted it towards the Fraser (Suttles, *Northwest Coast*, 455). According to Horatio Webb's observance of Mr Vedder's lost diary, on 8 March 1873 the Chilliwack River in freshet began taking over the bed of Vedder Creek, which in recent memory had been a small stream flowing into Sumas Lake (Chilliwack Archives [CHA], Webb, "History of the Chilukweyuk River").
8 National Archives of Canada (NAC), RG89, vol. 533, file 841, P.A. Carson, DLS, "Report on the Sumas Dyking Project," 2 July 1912, 17.
9 Marian Smith, "The Nooksack, the Chilliwack, and the Middle Fraser," 340, map; Valerie Cameron, "Geomorphic History," 111.
10 The Nooksack flooded the western edge of Sumas Prairie in 1986, 1989, and 1990. The Americans refuse to build dykes or dredge deeply, insisting that the Nooksack is simply following a natural course.
11 Valerie Cameron, "Geomorphic History," 111.
12 Ten registered archaeological sites ring the Sumas Lake region. Gordon Mohs, in his "Sumas Lake: Review of Reclamation & Native Use" (Stó:lō Tribal Council Collection [STCC]), notes that "undoubtedly there are many more as a systematic inventory of the area has never been conducted."
13 Arthur White, *Water Powers of B.C*, 45, 233. The book also reports that the lake is six miles long and four miles wide at nine foot elevation.
14 Cronon, "Kennecott Journey," in Cronon, Miles, and Gitlin, *Under an Open Sky*, 35.

15 According to Ned Johnson, curator in ornithology and professor of integrative biology, the museum holds fifty-nine specimens of birds and three specimens of mammals taken by the celebrated naturalist Allan Brooks in the Sumas Lake region.

16 *Funk & Wagnalls Standard College Dictionary.*

17 Simmons, *Environmental History*, 118.

18 Ibid.

19 In the interwar years when Sumas Lake was drained, the Dutch were embarking on one of their more ambitious projects, the dyking and drainage of the Zuider Zee; in Britain, where preservationists were calling for the drainage of the Wash to boost national morale, the Land Drainage Act of 1930 attempted to improve the Fenland artificial drainage system.

20 In discursive and political networks, the story of the Fens drainage certainly travelled. The British planner Thomas Adams, who worked on the Commission of Conservation, urged the drainage of Canadian marshes after the British model, asserting that "large sections of the best land in England, which is to-day producing the finest market garden crops, especially in the Fens of Lincolnshire and Cambridgeshire, have been reclaimed by drainage" (Adams, *Commission of Conservation Canada*, 9).

21 Regional District of Fraser Cheam Archive (RDFCA), Ward and McPhee, *Wetlands of the Fraser Lowland*, 1. Geraldine Irby reports that 70 per cent of the wetlands in British Columbia and Washington State have been lost (Irby, "Wetlands," 7).

22 Brooks, "Birds of the Chilliwack District," 29.

23 Cited in Ramsey, *Five Corners*, 12. See also UBCSPE, McDonald, "Journal of Fort Langley," 87–94.

24 Ibid., 15.

25 Stanley, *Mapping the Frontier*, 76.

26 Ibid., 77.

27 Curtis, *The Mosquitoes of British Columbia*, 3.

28 UBCSPE, Lord, *The Naturalist in Vancouver Island and B.C.*, 1:319.

29 Stanley, *Mapping the Frontier*, 61.

30 BCARS, Add. MSS 700, F.W. Laing, "Colonial Farm Settlers on Mainland B.C., 1858–71."

31 Cited in Stanley, *Mapping the Frontier*, 32, ftn. See also UBCSPE, Lord, *The Naturalist in Vancouver Island and B.C.*, 2:64.

32 Beldam, "Sumas Prairie," 32.

33 Duff, *The Upper Stalo Indians of the Fraser Valley*, 69, 77.

34 Coqualeetza Archives (CA), "Upper Stalo Fraser Valley Plant Gathering."

35 Marian Smith, "The Nooksack," 332; Ruby, *A Guide to Indian Tribes of the Pacific Northwest*, 153.

36 UBCSPE, Lord, *The Naturalist in Vancouver Island and B.C.*, 2:64.

37 Cited in Leach, *Waterfowl on a Pacific Estuary*, 56.

38 Ibid.

39 CA, Ware and Phillips, "Sumas Lake," in "Stó:lō History Fieldnotes," 28.

40 Cited in Leach, *Waterfowl on a Pacific Estuary*, 22.

41 Ibid.

42 B.C. Archives and Record Services (BCARS), British Columbia, *Papers Connected with the Indian Land Question*, 43.

43 British Columbia, Surveyor General Branch, Plan 31T1, "Reserves Laid Off for Government Purposes," W. McColl, 16 May 1864.

44 BCARS, British Columbia, *Papers Connected with the Indian Land Question*, 44.

45 Tennant, *Aboriginal Peoples*, 43.

46 Fisher, *Contact and Conflict*, 161.

47 Tennant, *Aboriginal Peoples*, 43.

48 Leach, *Waterfowl on a Pacific Estuary*, 57.

49 Duff, *The Upper Stalo Indians of the Fraser Valley*, 28.

50 Aylechootlook, on Capt. Jemmett's 1881 survey (Canada, CLSR, *Field Book* BC 9).

51 BCARS, British Columbia, *Papers Connected with the Indian Land Question*, 57.

52 See, for instance, the 1874 petition of the Lower Fraser chiefs: "Sumaas (at the junction of Sumass River and Fraser) with a population of seventeen families, is allowed 43 acres of meadow for their hay, and 32 acres of dry land" (Canada, *Special Joint Committee*, 103).

53 McFarland, "Indian Reserve Cut-Offs," 38.

54 The Sumas tribe was listed with 126 people and 78 cattle on six reserves (NA, RG10, vol. 10012, "Stalo Bands List. An Early Census of the Stó:lō Villages, Yale to Katzie"). See also CA, "Stó:lō Source Book," 159–63.

55 Fisher, *Contact and Conflict*, 189.

56 Harris, "Lower Mainland," 59.

57 BCARS, *Guide to the Province of British Columbia for 1877–8*, 117–25.

58 British Columbia, Sumas Dyking Act, *Statutes of B.C.*, 1878, c. 6.

59 NA, RG10, vol. 7538, file 27150-8-20, Sproat to Derby, 26 December 1878.

60 Ibid., Derby to chief commissioner of Indian affairs, 31 December 1878.
61 Ibid., Sproat to superintendent general of Indian affairs, 27 January 1879.
62 Ibid., 25 January 1879.
63 NA, RG10, vol. 7538, file 27150-8-20, Walkem to Macdonald, 6 March 1879.
64 Duane Thomson, "A History of the Okanagan," 138.
65 NA, RG10, vol. 7538, file 27150-8-20, Walkem to superintendent general of Indian affairs, 17 March 1879.
66 Ibid., Vankoughnet to Sproat, 3 April 1879.
67 Ibid., Vankoughnet to Macdonald, 3 April 1879.
68 Canada, CLSR, *Field Book*, BC 9.
69 NA, RG10, vol. 7538, file 27150-8-20, Sproat to Vankoughnet, 17 March 1879.
70 NA, RG15, vol. 778, file 540515, "Extract from a Report of the Committee of the Honorable, the Privy Council, approved by His Excellency on the 21st October, 1896." The dominion actually had title to the lake bottom, since the province administered water rights in the Railway Belt. However, this issue is controversial. For further reading, see Notzke, *Aboriginal Peoples and Natural Resources in Canada*, 15.
71 Matsqui-Sumas-Abbotsford archives (MSA), Louis Sam Papers.
72 Cook, "Early Settlement in the Chilliwack Valley," 12.
73 NA, RG10, vol. 7538, file 27150-8-20, memorandum, S.Bray to deputy minister of Indian affairs, 19 January 1907; ibid., G.W. Chadsey to Daly, minister of the interior, 6 June 1895.
74 CHA, Add. MSS 27, file 13, Charles Evans, "Reminiscences of the Fraser River Indian."
75 CHA, Add. MSS 27, files 1–2, Charles Evans, "Account Book and Stock Breeding Records, 1896–1904." See Newell's *Tangled Webs of History* for more information on this general trend. Newell analyses the increasing obstacles to Native participation in the Pacific Coast fishing industry.
76 Neil Smith Collection (NSC), Barbara Beldam, "May to December (Looking Backwards)," 57.
77 Beldam, "Sumas Prairie," 34.
78 NA, RG10, vol. 7538, file 27150-8-20, W.C. Bowman to deputy superintendent of Indian affairs, 2 March 1910.
79 Wood, Dang, and Ellis, *The Insects and Arachnids of Canada*, part 6, *The Mosquitoes of Canada*, 251.
80 Hearle, "The Mosquitoes of the Lower Fraser Valley and Their Control," 27–41.

81 Curtis, *The Mosquitoes of B.C.*, 6. See also Belton, *The Mosquitoes of British Columbia*, 19 and Andy Tomec, "Valley Braces for Mosquito Outbreak," *Chilliwack Times*, 17 April 1990.

82 Oliver Wells, *Vocabulary of Native Words in the Halkomelem Language*, 27.

83 CHA, Add. MSS 435, Effie Jane Bellrose, "Diary, January 1898 to December 1902." See also CHA, Add. MSS 435, Myrtle Ferguson.

84 Beldam, "Sumas Prairie," 34.

85 Duff, *The Upper Stó:lō Indians of the Fraser Valley*, 82, 96.

86 DDT is now banned in North America, but the United States exports as much as 18 million kilograms each year for use in developing countries (Israelson, *Silent Earth*, 34).

87 MSA, Foulds, "The Land Beneath the Lake," 7; Ormsby, *British Columbia: A History*, 407; Barman, *The West beyond the West*, 241.

88 Brooks, "Birds of the Chilliwack District," 30.

89 Leach, *Waterfowl on a Pacific Estuary*, 61. See also Laing, *Allan Brooks: Artist Naturalist*.

90 Museum of Vertebrate Zoology, collection holdings data (not viewed personally and not to be considered primary data) at the University of California Berkeley, printed 16 March 1994. Brooks notes in "Birds of the Chilliwack District" that he sent "numbers" of semi-palmated sandpipers "to the large eastern collections." The semipalmated sandpiper is also extinct in the Chilliwack/Sumas district, according to naturalist Denis Knopf in his 1992 list of "Birds of the Chilliwack District, B.C."

91 Brooks, "Birds of the Chilliwack District," 34.

92 Cited in "Stó:lō Source Book," 200 (CA). See also "Rod Fishing Is Being Injured," *Chilliwack Progress*, 30 April 1913.

93 Glavin, "An Ancient Enigma and a Death on the River," 7.

94 Cited in "Stó:lō Source Book," 199. (CA), and Glavin, *A Ghost in the Water*, 43. See also *Chilliwack Progress*, 26 April 1905, and "The Government Seizure," *Chilliwack Progress*, 3 May 1905.

95 Foster, *Working for Wildlife*, 12.

96 NA, RG10, vol. 7545, file 29153, MacAdam to minister of Indian affairs, 12 January 1904, and Devlin to Vowell, 6 February 1903.

97 Under Interim Report no. 17, the Maclure Tramway of the Victoria, Vancouver and Eastern Railway & Navigation Company claimed a 32.6-acre right-of-way from the Upper Sumas Reserve in the New Westminster Agency. Abandoned in the 1940s, the land was sold and subdivided, without compensation (Ware, *The Lands We Lost*, 21).

98 NA, RG10, vol. 7535, file 26153-1.

99 Leach, *Waterfowl on a Pacific Estuary*, 32.

100 Foster, *Working for Wildlife*, 140. See also the Migratory Birds Convention Act, *Statutes of Canada*, 1917, 8 Geo. 5, c. 18.

101 Foster, *Working for Wildlife*, 141. See also Northwest Game Act, *Statutes of Canada*, 1917, 8 Geo. 5, c. 36.

102 Titley, *A Narrow Vision*, 54.

103 Ormsby, *British Columbia: A History*, 407.

104 Jim Bowman, "Few as Popular as E.D. Barrow," *Chilliwack Times*, 24 November 1992.

105 MSA, Sumas Lake Papers, *Abbotsford Post*, 18 July 1918.

106 *The Fraser Valley Record*, 5 September 1918.

107 MSA, Sumas Lake Papers, *Abbotsford Post*, 13 September 1918.

108 Belton, *The Mosquitoes of British Columbia*, 30.

109 NA, RG89 vol. 269, file 3594, Desbarats to Department of Interior, 20 October 1917.

110 Ibid., S. Maber to Desbarats, 8 November 1917.

111 BCARS, GR929, box 52, file 1, J.A. Motherwell, chief inspector of fisheries, to commissioner, Land Settlement Board, 11 August 1922. The Land Settlement Board answered, "Your wire eleventh. re passage salmon into Sumas Lake. Our Engineer Sinclair fully authorized to take any possible action."

112 Brooks, "Birds of the Chilliwack District," 29. Allan Brooks changed his opinion in 1945 after visiting the bird sanctuary established by farmer-historian Oliver Wells in Sardis. He told Wells that "duck shooting might be increased by establishing areas of complete protection for holding birds in the valley. Otherwise (there is) not enough water for loafing grounds" (Leach, *Waterfowl on a Pacific Estuary*, 25).

113 Cited in Robert J. McKinnon, "Mosquito Land: 1808–1980," prepared for the Chilliwack Museum and Historical Society, July 1985 (RDFCA). See also *Chilliwack Progress*, 14 August 1919.

114 Hearle, *Mosquitoes of the Lower Fraser Valley*, 16.

115 Hearle, "A New Mosquito from British Columbia," 4. Hearle later suggested that it was synonymous with *Aedes mutatus dyar* (*Mosquitoes of the Lower Fraser Valley*); and in Matheson's *Handbook of the Mosquitoes of North America*, vol. 5, it is listed under *Aedes increpitus dyar* at a spot where, in my borrowed edition, a library patron has placed two four-leaf clovers.

116 Hearle, Mosquitoes of the Lower Fraser Valley, 13.

117 Ibid., 81.

118 The term "ecosystem" was developed in 1935 by the British ecologist A.G. Tansley.

119 Curtis, *The Mosquitoes of B.C.*, 4.

120 Vancouver *Province*, 24 November 1919.

121 NA, RG89, vol 269, file 3594, Drake to minister, Department of the Interior, 15 February 1923.

122 NA, RG10, vol. 7886, file 36153–13, Ditchburn, chief inspector of Indian agencies, to secretary, Department of Indian Affairs, 31 October 1923. The Land Settlement Board finally applied for the purchase of 26.96 acres of the Aylechootlook reserve in December 1923 and paid $188.72 ($7.00 per acre), the valuation stipulated by the Department of Indian Affairs.

123 CHA, Acc. 992.35, "Cultus Lake Park Board General Correspondence, 1924–1926."

124 Beldam, "Sumas Prairie," 36.

125 As hop pickers, Stó:lō women, men, and children were integral to the success of the hop industry. By the 1940s, automated machinery was replacing their labour. See Keith Thor Carlson and John Lutz, "Stó:lō People and the Development of the B.C. Wage Labour Economy," in Carlson, *You Are Asked to Witness*, 118–19.

CHAPTER THREE

1 Jody Cameron, "A Longer View: Preserve Present, Future," *Chilliwack Progress Weekender*, 4 June 1993.

2 Mrs M, interview at her home, 8 March 1994.

3 Mr G, lake bottom tour, 9 March 1994.

4 Mrs M, lake bottom tour, 22 March 1994.

5 Mr H, interview at his home, 21 July 1994.

6 Cronon, "A Place for Stories," 1375.

7 Cruikshank, "Oral Traditions and Written Accounts," 26.

8 Mrs J, untaped conversation at the Sumas Days festival, July 1994.

9 Casey Wells, "Old Chilliwack River North" (Tape, School District 33, *ca* 1968).

10 UBC Special Collections (UBCSPE), Lord, *The Naturalist in Vancouver Island and B.C.*, 315.

11 Chief Ned. See B.C. Archives and Record Services (BCARS), Add. MSS 1056, British Columbia, *Royal Commission on Indian Affairs*, 155.

12 Siemens, *Lower Fraser Valley*, 38.

13 Cronon, "A Place for Stories," 1376.

14 George White, "The Development of the Eastern Fraser Valley," 290.

15 BCARS, GR929, box 48, file 3, W.S. Latta, director, Land Settlement Board, "Record of Events: Sumas," 31 December 1926, 37. Latta writes: "Looking over the project now that it is completed, and taking into consideration its past history and future prospects, there can be no question of the tremendously beneficial effects this reclamation work will have on the Fraser Valley in particular and the Province in general. Where 4 years ago there lay an 8000 acre area of mud and water too shallow for navigation and too deep for the comfort of the occasional duck hunter who was the only one to get even a few days use out of it, and which formed probably the finest breeding ground for mosquitoes in the Dominion of Canada, there now exists as fine a stretch of farming country as the eye could wish to see; excellent soil, level land, ample water supply for stock and domestic purposes, splendid system of drainage, close to transportation, less than 50 miles from an urban community of nearly 300,000 people, combined with an equable climate and adequate rainfall. It is difficult to conceive of any farm lands more favorably situated on the North American Continent."

16 "Drainage of Sumas Lake: The Dream That Took 50 Years," *Valley Magazine*, 26 May 1982.

17 Hutchison, *The Fraser*, 5.

18 Ibid., 12.

19 Ormsby, *British Columbia: A History*, 407.

20 Barman, *The West beyond the West*, 241.

21 Worster, *Under Western Skies*, 6.

22 Hill-Tout, *The Salish People*, 3:14.

23 See, for example, Cruikshank, *Life Lived Like a Story*, and Basso, *Western Apache Language and Culture*.

24 Coqualeetza Archives (CA), Lerman, "Lower Fraser Indian Folktales, 1950–51," Gus Commodore, "Thunderbird I (Sumas Lake)," transcript.

25 For one version of the story, see Oliver Wells, *The Chilliwacks and Their Neighbours*, 88.

26 CA, Lerman, "Lower Fraser Indian Folktales," Agnes James, "Mink I: 3rd Version (Kilgard)," transcript.

27 See the HyperCard stack for the full transcript.

28 CA, Lerman, "Lower Fraser Indian Folktales," Gus Commodore, "Mosquito I (Sumas Lake)." The Mosquito Story is now also in storybook form, told by Dolly Felix and edited by LaVerne

Adams for the Coqualeetza Education Training Centre. There is a lake in this version, but it is unnamed.

29 CA, Lerman, "Lower Fraser Indian Folktales," Mrs Harry Uslick, "The Drought (Kilgard)."
30 BCARS, Sound and Moving Image Division, Imbert Orchard, "Mr. Joe Louie" (4/1/67), cassettes 437–1 & 2.
31 Oliver Wells, *The Chilliwacks and Their Neighbours*, 40.
32 Ibid., 50.
33 CA, Lerman, "Lower Fraser Indian Folktales," Mrs Harry Uslick, "The Drought (Kilgard)."
34 Aram Yengoyan, cited in Stock, "Reading, Community and a Sense of Place," 323.
35 Cronon, "A Place for Stories," 1370.

CHAPTER FOUR

1 Bates, *Forest and the Sea*, 175.
2 Bates, *Natural History of Mosquitoes*.
3 Matheson, *Handbook of the Mosquitoes of North America*, 191.
4 Latour, *We Have Never Been Modern*, 29.
5 Joyce, *Ulysses*, 649–50.
6 Latour, *We Have Never Been Modern*, 130.
7 Bates, *Natural History of Mosquitoes*, 282.
8 Ibid., 41.
9 See M.C. Healey, in Dorcey, *Water in Sustainable Development*, i.
10 Carroll, *Alice's Adventures in Wonderland and Through the Looking-Glass*, 180.

Bibliography

Sources are listed, when possible, by the name of the archive from which they were gathered. Oral interviews conducted during this project will be archived according to the wishes of the participants, as stipulated by the terms of my agreement with the University of British Columbia's "Ethical Review of Activities Involving Human Subjects in Questionnaries, Interviews, Observations, Testing, Video & Audio Tapes."

ARCHIVAL SOURCES

BRITISH COLUMBIA ARCHIVES AND RECORD SERVICES
British Columbia. *Inspector of Dykes, 1916–1975.* GR 1569.
– *Land Settlement Board, 1916–1967.* GR 929.
– *Papers Connected with the Indian Land Question, 1850–1875.* Victoria: Government Printer, 1875. Reprint, 1987.
– *Royal Commission on Indian Affairs for the Province of B.C., 1913–1915.* Union of B.C. Indian Chiefs. Add. MSS 1056.
– *Sumas Dyking District Commission, 1929.* GR 1089.
Canada. *Commission on Indian Affairs in General, 1913–1915.* B-1457.
Guide to the Province of B.C. for 1877–8. Victoria: T.N. Hibben & Co., 1877.
Laing, F.W. "Colonial Farm Settlers on Mainland B.C., 1858–71." Add. MSS 700.

Oral History
Orchard, Imbert. "Mr. Joe Louie" (4/1/67), 437–1 & 2. Sound and Moving Image Division.

CHILLIWACK ARCHIVES
Beldam (Bowman), Barbara. "Chilliwack Lake and Beyond." Acc. 988.82.
Bellrose, Effie Jane. "Diary, January 1898 to December 1902." Add. MSS 435.
"Cultus Lake Park Board General Correspondence, 1924–26." Acc. 992.35.
Evans, Charles H. "Account Book and Stock Breeding Records, 1896–1904." Add. MSS 27, files 1, 2.
– "Reminiscences of the Fraser River Indian." Add. MSS 27, file 13.
Webb, Horatio. "History of the Chilukweyuk River with the Vedder and Luckacuck as I Saw Them in 1870."
Oral Histories
Myrtle Ferguson. Add. MSS 435.
Charlie Power. Add. MSS 401.
Stanley Webb. Add. MSS 408.

CITY OF VANCOUVER ARCHIVES
Oral History
Mrs Thomas Fraser York, Huntingdon, B.C., 1945. Add. MSS 54, vol. 13.

COQUALEETZA ARCHIVES
Duff, Wilson. "Fieldnotes." 1950–52.
Felix, Dolly. "The Mosquito Story," ed. LaVerne Adams. Coqualeetza Education Training Centre, 1979.
Lerman, Norman. "Lower Fraser Indian Folktales, 1950–51." Unpublished transcript. Coqualeetza Education Training Centre.
Map of Stó:lō Lands. Coqualeetza Education Training Centre, 1982.
"Stó:lō Source Book: A Documentary of the Stó:lō People 1800–1970." Coqualeetza Education Training Centre.
"Upper Stó:lō Fraser Valley Plant Gathering." Coqualeetza Education Training Centre, 1981.
Ware, Reuben, and Albert Phillips. "Stó:lō History Fieldnotes." Coqualeetza Education Training Centre, 1976–1979.

MATSQUI-SUMAS-ABBOTSFORD MUSEUM SOCIETY ARCHIVES
Foulds, Kris. "Land beneath the Lake." MSA Museum Society, 1991.
Louis Sam Papers. SAM.
Sumas Lake Papers. SAM.
Oral Histories
George Ferguson. AH98.
Edward Kelly. AH97.
Edith Lamson. AH105.
David Mathers. AH1.
Fritz Stromberg. AH100.

NATIONAL ARCHIVES OF CANADA
Canada. Department of Agriculture. RG17, vol. 1276.
– Department of Indian Affairs. *Central Registry Files, 1868–1970.* RG10, vols. 7535, 7538, 7545, 7886.
– Department of Interior. RG15, vol. 778.
– Department of Interior. Water Resources Branch. RG89, vols. 269, 270, 273, 274, 275, 575.
– National Research Council. *Report of the President and Financial Statement 1926–27.*

NEIL SMITH COLLECTION
Beldam, Barbara. *May to December (Looking Backwards).* Beldam, 1979.
Ida (Bowman) Campbell's autograph book. 1889.
Log of the *Argo.* 1897. Photostat.

REGIONAL DISTRICT OF FRASER CHEAM ARCHIVE
Furnell, Allan. "1989 Year End Report, Lower Mainland Regional District's Mosquito Control Program." Morrow and Associates Engineering Inc., 1989.
– "1990 Year End Report, Lower Mainland Regional District's Mosquito Control Program." Morrow and Associates Engineering Inc., 1990.
Furnell, Allan, and E.J. Jordan. "Lower Mainland Regional Districts' Mosquito Control Board." Morrow Engineering Ltd, 1987.
McKinnon, Robert J. "Mosquito Land: 1808–1930." Prepared for the Chilliwack Museum and Historical Society, July 1985.

"Summary of the 1992 Mosquito Control Program." Regional District of Fraser Cheam, 1992.

Ward, Peggy. *Wetlands of the Fraser Lowland, 1989: An Inventory.* Technical Report Series no. 146. Pacific and Yukon Region Canadian Wildlife Service, 1992.

Ward, Peggy, and Michael McPhee. *Wetlands of the Fraser Lowland: Ownership, Management and Protection Status, 1992.* Technical Report Series no. 200. Pacific and Yukon Region Canadian Wildlife Service, 1994.

SUMAS BAND COLLECTION

Hudson, Doug. "Coast Salish Reader." Draft copy. 1992.

STÓ:LŌ TRIBAL COUNCIL COLLECTION

Mohs, Gordon. "Stó:lō Origins." Report for the Stó:lō Tribal Council, September 1992.

– "Sumas Lake: Review of Reclamation & Native Use." For Roy Mussel (Stó:lō Tribal Council), [1980s].

– "The Upper Stó:lō Indians of British Columbia: An Ethno-Archaeological review." Report for the Alliance of Tribal Councils, February 1990.

UBC SPECIAL COLLECTIONS

Lord, John Keast. *At Home in the Wilderness: What to Do There and How to Do It: A Handbook for Travellers and Emigrants.* London: Hardwicke & Bogue, 1876.

– *The Naturalist in Vancouver Island and B.C.* London: Richard Bentley, 1866.

McDonald, Archibald [author from 16 October 1828 to end]. "Journal of Fort Langley Commencing with Voyage from Fort Vancouver June 27, 1827 to July 30, 1830." Photostat of original.

Sumas Dyking District Lands for Sale, Sumas Dyking Commissioners. Chilliwack and Victoria, January 1926.

ADDITIONAL GOVERNMENT PUBLICATIONS

Adams, Thomas. *Commission of Conservation Canada: Rural Planning and Development. A Study of Rural Conditions and Problems in Canada.* Ottawa, 1917.

Belton, Peter. *The Mosquitoes of British Columbia.* Handbook no. 41. Victoria: British Columbia Provincial Museum, 1983.

British Columbia. Royal Commission on Indian Affairs for the Province of British Columbia (McKenna-McBride Commission). *Report.* 4 vols. Victoria: Acme Press, 1916.

– Surveyor General Branch. Plan 31т1, "Reserves Laid Off for Government Purposes." W. McColl, 16 May 1864.

Canada. Canada Lands Surveys Records. *Field Book* вс9. W.S. Jemmett, 1881. (Yaalstrick Indian Reserve no. 1, Lakaway Indian Reserve no. 2, Timber Reserve no. 3, Aylechootlook Indian Reserve no. 5, Upper Sumas Indian Reserve no. 6, Sumas Indian Reserve no. 7)

– Department of Indian Affairs. Records. 1875–1916.

– *Special Joint Committee of the Senate and House of Commons Appointed to Inquire into the Claims of the Allied Indian Tribes of British Columbia, as Set Forth in Their Petition Submitted to Parliament in June 1926.* Ottawa: King's Printer, 1927.

Conference *Minutes* between the Allied Indian Tribes of B.C. and Dr D. Scott, 7–11 August 1923. Reprinted by NESIKA.

Curtis, Colin. *The Mosquitoes of British Columbia.* Occasional papers of the British Columbia Provincial Museum, no. 15. Victoria: Department of Recreation and Conservation, 1967.

Duff, Wilson. *The Upper Stalo Indians of the Fraser Valley, B.C.* Anthropology in British Columbia Memoir no. 1. Victoria: British Columbia Provincial Museum, 1952.

Fraser River Board. *Final Report of the Fraser River Board on Flood Control and Hydro-electric Power in the Fraser River Basin.* Victoria: Queen's Printer, 1963

Geological and Natural History Survey. *Report of Progress.* 1882, 1883, 1884.

Greater Vancouver Regional District Strategic Planning Department. *Livable Region Strategy: Proposals.* Burnaby, August 1993.

Hearle, Eric. *The Mosquitoes of the Lower Fraser Valley and Their Control.* National Research Council Report no. 17. Ottawa: King's Printer, 1926.

Hornby Island Official Community Plan. Victoria: Islands Trust, May 1992.

Laing, Hamilton M. *Allan Brooks: Artist Naturalist.* British Columbia Provincial Museum Special Publication no. 3. Victoria: British Columbia Provincial Museum, 1979.

Leach, Barry. *Waterfowl on a Pacific Estuary: A Natural History of Man and Waterfowl on the Lower Fraser River.* British Columbia Provincial Museum Special Publication no. 5. Victoria: British Columbia Provincial Museum, 1982.

McEachern, Alan. "Reasons for Judgement of the Honourable Chief Justice Alan McEachern." Supreme Court of British Columbia, no. 0843. Smithers Registry, 8 March 1991.

Orchard, Imbert. *Floodland and Forest.* Sound Heritage Series no. 37. Victoria: PABC Sound and Moving Division, 1983.

Turner, Nancy. *Thompson Ethnobotany: Knowledge and Usage of Plants by Thompson Indians of B.C.* Victoria: Royal British Columbia Museum, 1990.

United States. Army Engineer District. *Nooksack River: Floodplain Information Study.* Seattle and Washington, January 1964.

– Army Engineer District. *Sumas River Supplement: Floodplain Information Study.* Seattle and Washington, May 1967.

White, Arthur V. *Water Powers of British Columbia.* Dominion Commission of Conservation, 1919.

Wood, D.M., P.T. Dang, and R.A. Ellis. *The Insects and Arachnids of Canada.* Part 6, *The Mosquitoes of Canada, Diptera: Culicidae.* Ottawa: Research Branch, Agriculture Canada, 1979.

Wright, D. Frank. *Barrowtown Pump Station.* Abbotsford, B.C.: District of Abbotsford, 1993.

NEWSPAPERS/MAGAZINES

Abbotsford Post
Abbotsford, Sumas and Matsqui News
Chilliwack Museum & Historical Society Newsletter
Chilliwack Progress
Chilliwack Times
Day and Knight
Fraser Valley Record
Lynden Tribune
Valley Magazine
Vancouver Province
Vancouver Sun

THESES AND OTHER UNPUBLISHED SOURCES

Arnett, Terrance, C. "The Chilliwack Valley Continuum: A Search for a Canadian Land Ethic." M ARCH thesis, University of British Columbia, 1976.

Cameron, Valerie. "The Late Quaternary Geomorphic History of the Sumas Valley." MA thesis, Simon Fraser University, 1989.

Cook, Donna H. "Early Settlement in the Chilliwack Valley." MA thesis, University of British Columbia, 1979.

Gibbard, John E. "Early History of the Fraser Valley, 1808–1885." MA thesis, University of British Columbia, 1937.

Harris, Cole. "Voices of Disaster: Smallpox around the Strait of Georgia in 1782." Draft version, in possession of author, 1994.

Imus, H.R. "Land Utilization in the Sumas Lake District, British Columbia." MA thesis, University of Washington, 1948.

Keddie, Grant. "The Archaeology of Mosquito Victims: A Unique Settlement Pattern on the Lower Fraser River." British Columbia Provincial Museum, 1980.

Knopf, Denis. "Birds of the Chilliwack District, B.C." Sardis, B.C., 1992.

Lerman, Norman. "An analysis of Folktales of Lower Fraser Indians, British Columbia." MA thesis, University of Washington, 1952.

McFarland, Dana. "Indian Reserve Cut-Offs in British Columbia, 1912–1924: An Examination of Federal-Provincial Negotiations and Consultation with Indians." MA thesis, University of British Columbia, 1990.

McKinnon, Robert J. "Mosquito Land: 1808–1980." Paper prepared for the Chilliwack Museum and Historical Society, July 1985.

Riddett, Lyn. "Think Again: Communities Which Lose Their Memory: The Construction of History in Settler Societies." Paper, Northern Territory University, 1992.

Smith, Bob. "The Reclamation of the Sumas Lands." Paper, Fraser Valley College, 1982.

Sparrow, Leona. "Work Histories of a Coast Salish Couple." MA thesis, University of British Columbia, 1976.

Thomson, Duane. "A History of the Okanagan: Indians and Whites in the Settlement Era, 1860–1920." PHD thesis, University of British Columbia, 1985.

Tremaine, David G. "Indian and Pioneer Settlement of the Nooksack Lowland, Washington to 1890." Occasional Paper no. 4. Center for Pacific Northwest Studies, Western Washington State College, 1975.

Wells, Casey. "Old Chilliwack River North." Tape 35:06. School District 33, *ca* 1968.

BOOKS AND ARTICLES

Asch, Michael. *Home and Native Land: Aboriginal Rights and the Canadian Constitution.* Toronto: Methuen, 1984.

Atwood, Margaret. *Survival: A Thematic Guide to Canadian Literature.* Toronto: Anansi, 1972.

Barman, Jean. *The West beyond the West: A History of British Columbia.* Toronto: University of Toronto Press, 1991.

Barnes, Trevor, and James Duncan, eds. *Writing Worlds: Discourse, Text and Metaphor in the Representation of Landscape.* London and New York: Routledge, 1992.

Basso, Keith. *Western Apache Language and Culture: Essays in Linguistic Anthropology.* Tucson, Ariz.: University of Arizona Press, 1990.

Bates, Marston. *The Forest and the Sea: A Look at the Economy of Nature and the Ecology of Man.* New York: Random House, 1960.

– *Natural History of Mosquitoes.* New York: Macmillan, 1949.

Beldam, Barbara. "Sumas Prairie: A Mosaic of Memory." In *Making History: An Anthology of B.C.,* ed. Millicent Lindo. Victoria: Lindo, 1974.

Binney, Judith. "Maori Oral Narratives, Pakeha Written Texts: Two Forms of Storytelling." *New Zealand Journal of History* 21, no. 1 (April 1987): 16–28.

Bloch, Marc. *The Historian's Craft.* New York: Knopf, 1963.

Block, Bernard, and Robert Lee Scott, eds. *Methods of Rhetorical Criticism: A Twentieth-Century Perspective.* Detroit: Wayne State University Press, 1980.

Bowen, Lynne. *Boss Whistle: The Coal Miners of Vancouver Island Remember.* Lantzville, B.C.: Oolichan Books, 1982.

Brand, Stuart. *The Media Lab: Inventing the Future at M.I.T.* New York: Penguin Books, 1987.

Braudel, Fernand. *On History.* Chicago: University of Chicago Press, 1980.

– *The Mediterranean and the Mediterranean World in the Age of Phillip II*, Vols. 1, 2. New York: Harper & Row, 1973.

Brooks, Allan. "Birds of the Chilliwack District, B.C." *Auk* 34 (1917): 28–50.

Burgis, Mary, and Pat Morris. *The Natural History of Lakes.* Cambridge: Cambridge University Press, 1987.

Buttimer, Anne. "Nature, Water Symbols and the Human Quest for Wholeness." In *Dwelling, Place and Environment: Towards a Phenomenology of Person and World,* ed. David Seamon and Robert Mugerauer. New York: Columbia University Press, 1985.

Cail, Robert E. *Land, Man and the Law: The Disposal of Crown Lands in British Columbia, 1871–1913.* Vancouver: UBC Press, 1974.

Cameron, Laura, "A Lake Vanishes." *Pacific Current*, June 1995, 14–18.

Carlson, Keith, ed. *You Are Asked to Witness: The Stó:lō in Canada's Pacific Coast History.* Chilliwack, B.C.: Stó:lō Heritage Trust, 1997.

Carr, David. *Time, Narrative and History.* Bloomington: Indiana University Press, 1986.

Carroll, Lewis. *Alice's Adventures in Wonderland and Through the Looking-Glass.* New York: Grosset and Dunlap, n.d.

Cherrington, John. *The Fraser Valley: A History.* Madeira Park: Harbour, 1992.

Chomsky, Noam, interviewed by David Barsamian. *Chronicles of Dissent.* Vancouver: New Star Books, 1992.

Clifford, James, and George Marcus, eds. *Writing Culture: The Poetics and Politics of Ethnography: A School of American Research Advanced Seminar.* Berkeley: University of California Press, 1986.

Cronon, William. "A Place for Stories: Nature, History and Narrative." *Journal of American History* 78, no. 4 (March 1992): 1346–76.

– *Uncommon Ground: Towards Reinventing Nature.* New York: W.W. Norton, 1995.

Cronon, William, George Miles, and Jay Gitlin, eds. *Under an Open Sky: Rethinking America's Western Past.* New York: W.W. Norton, 1992.

Crosby, Thomas. *Among the An-ko-me-nums: Or Flathead Tribes of Indians of the Pacific Coast.* Toronto: William Briggs, 1907.

Cruikshank, Julie. "Getting the Words Right: Perspectives on Naming and Places in Athapaskan Oral History." *Arctic Anthropology*, 27, no. 1 (1990): 52–65.

– "Oral Traditions and Written Accounts: An Incident from the Klondike Gold Rush." *Culture* 9, no. 2 (1989): 25–31.

Cruikshank, Julie, with Angela Sidney, Kitty Smith, and Annie Ned. *Life Lived Like a Story: Life Stories of Three Yukon Native Elders.* Vancouver: UBC Press, 1992.

Davis, Wade. *Shadows in the Sun: Essays on the Spirit of Place.* Edmonton, Alta: Lone Pine, 1992.

Diamond, Irene, and Gloria Orenstein, eds. *Reweaving the World: The Emergence of Ecofeminism.* San Francisco: Sierra Club Books, 1990.

Dickason, Olive. *Canada's First Nations: A History of Founding Peoples from Earliest Times.* Toronto: McClelland & Stewart, 1992.

Dorcey, Anthony, ed. *Perspectives on Sustainable Development in Water Management*, vol 1. *Water in Sustainable Development: Exploring Our Common Future in the Fraser River Basin*, vol. 2. Westwater Research Centre, UBC, 1991.

"Environmental History: A Round Table." *Journal of American History* (special issue), 76, no. 4 (March 1990).

Faragher, John Mack. "The Frontier Trail: Rethinking Turner and Reimaging the Frontier Trail." *American Historical Review* 98, no. 1 (Feb 1993): 106–17.

Fawcett, Brian. *Cambodia: A Book for People Who Find Television Too Slow.* Vancouver: Talonbooks, 1986.

Fisher, Robin. *Contact and Conflict: Indian-European Relations in British Columbia, 1774–1890.* Vancouver: UBC Press, 1978.

Fisher, Robin, and Kenneth Coates, eds. *Out of the Background: Readings on Canadian Native History.* Toronto: Copp Clark Pitman, 1988.

Foster, Janet. *Working for Wildlife: The Beginning of Preservation in Canada.* Toronto: University of Toronto Press, 1978.

Foucault, Michel. *Language, Counter-Memory, Practice: Selected Essays and Interviews.* Ithaca, N.Y.: Cornell University Press, 1977.

– *Power/Knowledge: Selected Interviews and Other Writings 1972–1977.* New York: Pantheon Books, 1980.

Franklin, Ursula. *The Real World of Technology.* Concord, Ont.: Anansi, 1992.

– "Silence and the Notion of the Commons." *MusicWorks* 59 (Summer 1994): 38–42.

Fraser, Simon. *Letters and Journals, 1806–1808,* ed. W. Kaye Lamb. Toronto: Macmillan, 1960.

Frisch, Michael. *A Shared Authority: Essays on the Craft and Meaning of Oral and Public History.* Albany, N.Y.: State University of New York, 1990.

Frye, Northrop. "Conclusion." In *Literary History of Canada,* ed. Carl Klinck. Toronto: University of Toronto Press, 1965.

Fung, Richard. "Working through Cultural Appropriation." *Fuse* 16 nos. 5, 6 (Summer 1993): 16–24.

Funk & Wagnalls Standard College Dictionary. Toronto: Fitzhenry & Whiteside, 1978.

Gablik, Suzi. *The Reenchantment of Art.* New York: Thames and Hudson, 1992.

Galloway, Brent. *A Grammar of Upriver Halkomelem.* Berkeley: University of California Press, 1993.

Glavin, Terry. "An Ancient Enigma and a Death on the River." *Georgia Strait,* 3–10 December 1993, 7–9.

– *A Ghost in the Water.* Vancouver: New Star Books, 1994.

Gluck, Sherna Berger, and Daphne Patai, eds. *Women's Words: The Feminist Practice of Oral History.* New York: Routledge, 1991.

Goodman, Danny. *The Complete Hypercard Handbook.* Toronto: Bantam Books, 1987.

Goudie, Andrew. *The Human Impact on the Natural Environment.* London: Blackwell, 1988.

Grele, Ronald, ed. *International Annual of Oral History, 1990: Subjectivity and Multiculturalism in Oral History.* New York: Greenwood Press, 1992.

Hagopian, Patrick. "Oral Narratives: Secondary Revision and the Memory of the Vietnam War." *History Workshop Journal* 32 (Autumn 1991): 134–50.

Harris, Cole. "The Lower Mainland, 1820–81." In *Vancouver and Its Region*, ed. Graeme Wynn and Timothy Oke. Vancouver: UBC Press, 1992.

Hastrup, Kirsten, ed. *Other Histories*. London: Routledge, 1992.

Hayden, Delores. *The Power of Place: Urban Landscapes as Public History*. Cambridge, Mass.: MIT Press, 1995.

Hearle, Eric. "A New Mosquito from British Columbia." *Canadian Entomologist* 55, no. 5 (1923): 4, 265.

Hill-Tout, Charles. *The Salish People: The Local Contribution of Charles Hill-Tout*, ed. Ralph Maud. Vol. 3, *The Mainland Halkomelem*. Vancouver: Talonbooks, 1978.

Hiss, Tony. *The Experience of Place*. New York: Knopf, 1990.

Hofmeyr, Isabel. "Nterata/The Wire: Fences, Boundaries, Orality, Literacy." In *International Annual of Oral History, 1990: Subjectivity and Multiculturalism in Oral History*, ed. Ronald Grele. New York: Greenwood Press, 1992.

Hutchison, Bruce. *The Fraser*. Toronto: Clarke, Irwin, 1950.

Iggers, Georg G. "The Annales Tradition: French Historians in Search of History." In *New Directions in European Historiography*, ed. Georg Iggers and Norman Baker. Middletown, Conn.: Wesleyan University Press, 1975.

Innis, Harold Adams. *Empire and Communications*. Toronto: University of Toronto Press, 1972.

Irby, Geraldine. "Wetlands: How Can We Define – and Protect – Them?" *Sierra Report* 12, no. 4 (Winter 1993/94): 7.

Israelson, David. *Silent Earth: The Politics of Our Survival*. Markham, Ont.: Viking, 1990.

Jeffcott, P.R. *Nooksack Tales and Trails*. Ferndale, Wash.: Sedro-Woolley Courier-Times, 1949.

Joyce, James. *Ulysses*. London: Chancellor Press, 1993.

Kerr, Donald, and Deryck W. Holdsworth, eds. *Historical Atlas of Canada*. Vol. 3, *Addressing the Twentieth Century, 1891–1961*. Toronto: University of Toronto Press, 1990.

Klassen, Agatha. *Yarrow: A Portrait in Mosaic*. Yarrow: A.E. Klassen, 1976.

Klinck, Carl F., ed. *Literary History of Canada*. Toronto: University of Toronto Press, 1965.

Knight, Rolf. *Indians at Work: An Informal History of Native Labour in British Columbia, 1858–1930*. Vancouver: New Star Books, 1978.

Kroker, Arthur. *Technology and the Canadian Mind: Innis/McLuhan/Grant*. Montreal: New World Perspectives, 1984.

Kruger, Barbara, ed. *Remaking History*. Dia Art Foundation. Discussions in Contemporary Culture, no. 4. Seattle: Bay Press, 1989.

LaCapra, Dominick. *History and Criticism*. Ithaca, N.Y.: Cornell University Press, 1985.

– "Rethinking Intellectual History and Reading Texts." *History and Theory* 12, no. 3 (1980): 245–76.

Landow, George. *Hypertext: The Convergence of Contemporary Critical Theory and Technology.* Baltimore: Johns Hopkins University Press, 1992.

Latour, Bruno. *We Have Never Been Modern*, trans. Catherine Porter. Cambridge: Harvard University Press, 1993.

Lefebvre, Henri. *The Production of Space.* Oxford: Blackwell, 1991.

Leonoff, Cyril. *An Enterprising Life: Leonard Frank.* Vancouver: Talonbooks, 1990.

Lerman, Norman. *Legends of the River People*, ed. Betty Keller. Vancouver: November House, 1976.

Limerick, Patricia Nelson. *The Legacy of Conquest: The Unbroken Past of the American West.* New York: Norton, 1987.

Lowenthal, David. *The Past Is a Foreign Country.* Cambridge: Cambridge University Press, 1985.

McClintock, Anne. *Imperial Leather: Race, Gender and Sexuality in the Colonial Contest.* New York: Routledge, 1995.

MacGregor, Gaile. *The Wacousta Syndrome: Explorations in the Canadian Langscape.* Toronto: University of Toronto Press, 1985.

McLuhan, Marshall. *The Medium Is the Message: An Inventory of Effects.* New York: Bantam Books, 1967.

Mander, Jerry. *In the Absence of the Sacred: The Failure of Technology and the Survival of the Indian Nations.* San Francisco: Sierra Club Books, 1991.

Massey, Doreen. "A Place Called Home?" In *Space, Place and Gender.* Cambridge: Polity Press, 1994.

Matheson, Richard. *Handbook of the Mosquitoes of North America.* Vol. 5. New York: Comstock, 1944.

Maud, Ralph. *B.C. Indian Myth and Legend: A Short Survey of Myth-Collecting and a Survey of Published Texts.* Vancouver: Talonbooks, 1982.

Meyrowitz, Joshua. *No Sense of Place.* New York: Oxford University Press, 1985.

Miall, David, ed. *Metaphor: Problems and Perspectives.* Brighton: Harvester Press, 1982.

Mumford, Lewis. *The Myth of the Machine: Technics and Human Development.* New York: Harcourt, Brace & World, 1967.

Nash, Roderick. *Wilderness and the American Mind.* New Haven: Yale University Press, 1982.

Newell, Dianne. *Tangled Webs of History: Indians and the Law in Canada's Pacific Coast Fisheries.* Toronto: University of Toronto Press, 1993.

North, Margaret, and J.M. Teversham. "The Vegetation of the Lower Fraser, Serpentine and Nicomekl Rivers, 1859 to 1890." *Syesis* 17 (1984): 47–65.

Notzke, Claudia. *Aboriginal Peoples and Natural Resources in Canada.* York: Captus University Publications, 1994.

Ong, Walter. *Orality and Literacy: The Technologizing of the Word.* London: Methuen, 1982.

Ormsby, Margaret. *British Columbia: A History.* Toronto: Macmillan, 1958.

Parkes, Don, and Nigel Thrift, eds. *Times, Spaces and Places: A Chronogeographic Perspective.* Chichester: John Wiley, 1980.

Parr, Joy. *The Gender of Breadwinners: Women, Men and Change in Two Industrial Communities, 1880–1950.* Toronto: University of Toronto Press, 1990.

Portelli, Alessandro. "The Peculiarities of Oral History." *History Workshop Journal* 12 (Autumn 1981): 96–107.

Postman, Neil. *Technopoly: The Surrender of Culture to Technology.* Toronto: Vintage Books, 1993.

Pred, Allan. *Making Histories and Constructing Human Geographies: The Local Transformation of Practice, Power Relations, and Consciousness.* Boulder: Westview Press, 1990.

Prigogine, Ilya. *Order Out of Chaos: Man's New Dialogue with Nature.* Toronto: Bantam Books, 1984.

Prince, Hugh C. "Real, Imagined and Abstract Worlds of the Past." In *Progress in Geography: International Reviews of Current Research.* Vol. 3, ed. C. Board, R. Chorley, P. Haggett, and D. Stoddart. New York: St Martin's Press, 1971.

Ramsey, Bruce. *Five Corners: The Story of Chilliwack.* Vancouver: Agency Press, 1975.

Random House Webster's College Dictionary, ed. Robert Costello. New York: Random House, 1991.

Rheingold, Howard. *The Virtual Community: Homesteading on the Electronic Frontier.* Reading, Mass.: Addison-Wesley, 1993.

Ricoeur, Paul. *Time and Narrative.* Vols. 1, 3. Chicago: University of Chicago Press, 1984, 1988.

Ridington, Robin. *Little Bit Know Something: Stories in a Language of Anthropology.* Vancouver: Douglas & McIntyre, 1990.

Rifkin, Jeremy, with Ted Howard. *Entropy: A New World View.* New York: Viking Press, 1980.

Riggins, Loretta. *Heart of the Fraser Valley: Memories of an Era Past.* Clearbrook, B.C.: Clearbrook, Matsqui Centennial Society, 1991.

Ritchie, Carson. *Insects: The Creeping Conquerors.* New York: Elsevier-Dutton, 1979.

Rosaldo, Renato. "Doing Oral History." *Social Analysis* 4 (September 1980): 89–98.

Roth, Lottie Roeder. *History of Whatcom County.* Chicago: Pioneer Historical Publishing, 1926.

Ruby, Robert. *A Guide to the Indian Tribes of the Pacific Northwest.* Norman: Unversity of Oklahoma Press, 1986.

Sacks, Sheldon, ed. *On Metaphor.* Chicago: University of Chicago Press, 1979.

Samuel, Raphael. "Local History and Oral History." *History Workshop Journal* 1 (Spring 1976): 191–207.

Schiebinger, Londa. *Nature's Body: Gender and the Making of Modern Science.* Boston: Beacon Press, 1993.

Scott, Joan. "The Campaign against Political Correctness." *Radical History Review* 54 (Fall 1992): 59–79.

Shibles, Warren. *Essays on Metaphor.* Whitewater, Wisc.: The Language Press, 1972.

Shields, Rob. *Places on the Margin: Alternative Geographies of Modernity.* London: Routledge, 1991.

Siemens, Alfred, ed. *Lower Fraser Valley: Evolution of a Cultural Landscape.* Vancouver: Tantalus, 1968.

Simmons, I.G. *Environmental History: A Concise Introduction.* Oxford: Blackwell, 1993.

Slotkin, Richard. *The Fatal Environment: The Myth of the Frontier in the Age of Industrialization 1800–1890.* New York: Atheneum, 1985.

Smith, Allan. "The Writing of British Columbia History." *BC Studies* 45 (Spring 1980): 73–101.

Smith, Marian. "The Nooksack, the Chilliwack and the Middle Fraser." *Pacific Northwest Quarterly* 41, no. 4 (October 1950): 330–41.

Snyder, Gary. *The Practice of the Wild: Essays.* San Francisco: North Point Press, 1990.

Stanley, George F.G., ed. *Mapping the Frontier: Charles Wilson's Diary of the Survey of the 49th Parallel, 1858–1862, while Secretary of the British Boundary Commission.* Seattle: Unversity of Washington Press, 1970.

Stegner, Wallace. *Wolf Willow: A History, a Story, and a Memory of the Last Plains Frontier.* New York: Penguin, 1990.

Steiner, Dieter, and Markus Nauser, eds. *Human Ecology: Fragments of Anti-Fragmentary Views of the World.* London: Routledge, 1993.

Stock, Brian. "Reading, Community and a Sense of Place." In *Place, Culture and Representation*, ed. James Duncan and David Ley. London: Routledge, 1993.

Struever, Nancy. *The Language of History in the Renaissance.* New Jersey: Princeton University Press, 1970.

Suttles, Wayne. "Space and Time, Wind and Tide: Some Halkomelem Modes of Classification." In Suttles, *Coast Salish Essays.* Vancouver: Talonbooks, 1987.

– ed. *Northwest Coast.* Vol. 7 of *Handbook of North American Indians.* Washington, D.C.: Smithsonian Institution Press, 1990.

Tennant, Paul. *Aboriginal Peoples and Politics: The Indian Land Question in British Columbia, 1849–1989.* Vancouver: UBC Press, 1990.

Thomas, Keith. *Man and the Natural World: Changing Attitudes in England, 1500–1800.* London: Penguin Books, 1983.

Thompson, Paul. *The Voice of the Past: Oral History.* Oxford: Oxford University Press, 1988.

Titley, E. Brian. *A Narrow Vision: Duncan Campbell Scott and the Administration of Indian Affairs in Canada.* Vancouver: UBC Press, 1986.

Trigger, Bruce. *Natives and Newcomers: Canada's "Heroic Age" Reconsidered.* Montreal and Kingston: McGill-Queen's University Press, 1985.

Turner, Frederick. *Beyond Geography: The Western Spirit against the Wilderness.* New York: Viking Press, 1980.

Vansina, Jan. *Oral Tradition as History.* Madison, Wisc.: University of Wisconsin Press, 1985.

Ware, Reuben. *The Lands We Lost: A History of Cutoff Lands and Land Losses from Indian Reserves in British Columbia.* Vancouver: Union of B.C. Chiefs, 1974.

Wells, Oliver. *The Chilliwacks and Their Neighbours*, ed. Ralph Maud, Brent Galloway, and Marie Weeden. Vancouver: Talonbooks, 1987.

– *Vocabulary of Native Words in the Halkomelem Language.* Vedder, B.C.: Wells, 1965.

Where All Trails Meet. Matsqui, Sumas, and Abbotsford Centennial Society Historical Committee, 1959.

White, George. "The Development of the Eastern Fraser Valley." *British Columbia Historical Quarterly* 12, no. 4 (1948): 259–91.

White, Hayden. *The Content of the Form: Narrative Discourse and Historical Representation.* Baltimore: Johns Hopkins University Press, 1987.

– "Foucault Decoded: Notes from Underground." *History and Theory* 12, no. 1 (1973): 23–54.

– *Metahistory.* Baltimore: Johns Hopkins University Press, 1978.

– *Tropics of Discourse: Essays in Cultural Criticism.* Baltimore: Johns Hopkins University Press, 1978.

White, James. *When Words Lose Their Meaning: Constitutions and Reconstitutions of Language, Character and Community.* Chicago: University of Chicago Press, 1984.

White, Richard. *It's Your Misfortune and None of My Own: A History of the American West.* London: University of Oklahoma Press, 1991.

Williams, Raymond. *The Country and the City.* London: Hogarth Press, 1993.

Worster, Donald. *Under Western Skies: Nature and History in the American West.* New York: Oxford University Press, 1992.

– *The Wealth of Nature: Environmental History and the Ecological Imagination.* New York: Oxford University Press, 1993.

Wynn, Graeme, ed. *People, Places, Patterns, Processes: Geographical Perspectives on the Canadian Past.* Mississauga, Ont.: Copp Clark Pitman, 1990.

Wynn, Graeme, and Timothy Oke, eds. *Vancouver and Its Region.* Vancouver: UBC Press, 1992.

Young, Robert. *White Mythologies: Writing History and the West.* London: Routledge, 1990.

Index

Abbotsford, 13, 46, 76

Abbotsford Post, 67

Aboriginal title, 7, 14; and British Columbia, 29, 53, 55; and Joint Allotment Commission (1876–79), 53–7; and Special Committee hearing (1926), 38

Agassiz Experimental Farm, 68

Agricultural Land Reserve, 12

Alexander, Louie, 78, 80

Alice "in Wonderland," 6, 12, 94

Allied Indian Tribes of B.C., 34–6

Annance, François Noël, 49

archives, 41, 43, 94

Aylechootlook. *See* reserves

bald eagles, 50

Baldrey, Keith, 39

Barman, Jean, 84

Barrow, E.D., 67–8, 83

Barrowtown station, 89

Bates, Marston, 92–3

Beldam, Barbara (Bowman), 42–4; and B.C. Electric Railway, 67; on bluegrass, 50; and lake drainage, 74; on mosquitoes, 61; and poetry/politics, 59

Bellrose, Ms, 60

bittern, American, 51

Bloch, Marc, 18

boating, 18, 22, 23, 35. *See also* canoeing

border, Canada–U.S., 9, 46. *See also* International Boundary Commission

Bowman, Mary, 25

Bowman, Orion, 17, 25, 35

Bowman, W.C., 59

Brand, Stewart, 6

Braudel, Fernand, 13

British Columbia Electric Railway, 67; view of Sumas Lake from, 75

British Columbia Water Act, 36
British Privy Council, 36
Brooks, Allan, 19, 61–4, 107n90, 108n112
Brooks, W.E., 61
Buttimer, Anne, 13

Campbell, Ida (Bowman), 17, 95
Canadian bluegrass, 50
canoeing, 5, 21, 23, 37
Carr, David, 11
cattle, 24
Chad, Lake, 46
Chadsey, David, 26
Chilliwack, 16, 24, 38, 76
Chilliwack Museum and Historical Society, 21
Chilliwack Progress, 63
Chilliwack River, 46
Chilliwacks and Their Neighbors, The, 21
City of Vancouver Archives, 21
Cline, Alfred, 65
collecting, 61–4
colonialism: and fences, 27; and Simon Fraser,
    5; and historiography, 5, 43; and mosqui-
    toes, 67; and surveys, 51, 53; and Joseph
    Trutch, 27; and George Watts, 38, 39
Colonist, 29
Commission of Conservation, 46, 104n20
Commodore, Gus, 85–6
commons, 24, 26
community, 11, 43
computer technology. *See* electronic media
conservation, 46, 63, 66–9
Cooper, Amy, 87

Coqualeetza Residential School, 23, 88. *See
    also* residential schools
cranes, 49, 51, 67
Cronon, William, 48, 78
Cruikshank, Julie, 78
Cultus Lake, 18, 68, 74, 87
curlews, 67

DDT, 61, 107n86
deer, 21, 23
Department of Agriculture (dominion), 67, 69
Department of the Interior (dominion), 68, 72
Derby, Ellis Luther, 54–5
Deutsch, Sarah, 8
Dewdney, Edgar, 54
"Disappearing a Lake" HyperCard stack, 6
Dominion Entomological Service, 67–8. *See
    also* mosquitoes
Douglas, Governor Sir James, 51
drainage: in Canada, 43, 93; in Lower Main-
    land, 48; around the North Sea, 48. *See also*
    Sumas Lake drainage
ducks, 21–3, 43, 49, 66, 74
Duff, Wilson, 50
Dyar, H.G., 70

ecosystem, 72, 109n118
electronic media: in historiography, 6–14, 94.
    See also hypertext
Evans, Charles, 59

Fadden, Mrs, 23, 31
Farmers' Institute, 31

Fawcett, Brian, 13
fences, 24, 27. *See also* colonialism
Fens, the, 48, 104n20
fishing, 19, 23, 50; and net seizure, 63; of
    roundfish, 44; and G.M. Sproat's demands
    (1879), 57; and sturgeon weir, 50
flooding, 23, 24, 30. *See also* flood story
Floodland and Forest, 19
flood story, 86
flycatchers, 50
Fort Langley, 45
Foster, Janet, 63
Foucault, Michel, 13
Fraser, Simon, 3, 5
Fraser River: and "all living," 87; floodplain,
    46; gold rush, 44; as "prodigal waste of en-
    ergy," 83; and Sumas Lake waters, 5, 74;
    valley, 5, 34, 82; wetlands loss, 43. *See also*
    Stó:lō
frontier, 9
Frye, Northrop, 14

geese, 23, 49–51, 63
Glavin, Terry, 63
grazing, 24, 34, 49, 57
Great Britain, 44, 48. *See also* British Privy
    Council
Greeno, Clytie (Bowman), 17, 95
Greenpeace, 38, 39
grouse, 21
gyrfalcons, 57

Harcourt, Premier Mike, 38, 39

Harris, Cole, 27, 54
Harrison Lake, 18
Harrison River, 51
hawk, sharp-shinned, 62
Hearle, Eric, 70, 72
herons, 51
Hewitt, Gordon, 66, 68–9
Hicks Lake, 18
Hill-Tout, Charles, 84
History Circle, 38. *See also* oral history
Hofmeyr, Isabel, 27
homescape, 76, 86, 91
horses, 24
hunting, 23, 34, 38, 43, 49; Lakemount Marsh
    hunting grounds, 90. *See also* Treaty for In-
    ternational Protection of Migratory Birds
Hutchison, Bruce, 83, 85, 89
hypertext: conference at Yale (1994), 10; and
    creative responsibility, 9; and cultural ap-
    propriation, 9–10; definitions of, 6, 8; em-
    bodying theory, 7; "flowspace," 11; and
    frontiers, 9; and historiography, 6–14, 94;
    and HyperCard, 6

Indian Act, 38, 98n13
Innis, Harold Adams, 5
International Boundary Commission, 41, 44,
    49, 60, 82

James, Mrs Agnes, 86
Jemmett, Captain W.S., 57–8
Jim, Ke Ha, 31
Joint Allotment Commission (1876), 53–7

Joyce, James, 93
Joyce, Michael, 11

Kelleher, Mr and Mrs, 21
Kelly, Edward, 21, 24, 28
Kelly, Rev. Peter, 34, 36
Kilgard Reserve (Sumas no. 6). See reserves
knitting, 23
Kw'ekw'e'iqw, 86

Lakemount Marsh, 90
Landow, George, 8, 9
Land Settlement Board, 67, 69, 72, 83
Latour, Bruno, 5–6
Launders, J.B., 53
Legislative Assembly of B.C., Agricultural
    Committee of, 26
Lerman, Norman, 85–7
Lindeman Lake, 18
Lord, John Keast, 41, 49–51
Louie, Ed, 65
Louie, Joe, 65, 87–9

McColl, William, 51
McConnell, May and Myrtle, 20
Macdonald, Sir John A., 55
McEachern, Justice Allan, 7
McGregor Ridge, 90
McHalsie, Albert "Sonny," 85
McKenna-McBride Commission (1913–16),
    29–36, 66
Maitland, Miss, 20
mapping, 44–8, 53; hydrographic survey
(1912), 47; International Boundary Commis-
sion map (1869), 44, 45, 49–51; key map of
Sumas Reclamation Area (1919), 73; Lower
Fraser Valley mosquito-breeding areas
(1921), 70–2; rough diagram of "reserves
laid off" (1864), 52; Sumas Indian reserves
(1881–82), 57–8
marginal lands, 48, 72
Matheson, George, 36, 38
Matsqui, 55
Matsqui-Sumas-Abbotsford Museum Society,
    21
Matthews, Major J.S., 21
memory device, 88
memory tour, 78, 82
metaphor, 12
Miles, George, 19
milking, 24
Milo, Dan, 60, 87
Mink Story, 86
Mission, 70
mosquitoes: Aedes increpitus dyar (hewitti),
    70; Aedes sticticus, 50, 60; Aedes vexans,
    50, 60, 72, 91–3; aerial survey, 70–1, 93;
    and beauty, 61; and colonialism, 67; cop-
    ing manoeuvres, 60–1; and descriptions of
    Aboriginal technology, 50; and disease,
    60; and entomologists, 60, 66–72, 92–3;
    eradication of, 60–1, 66–73; as food for
    fish, 70; as food for insects, 61, 70; as food
    for wildfowl, 50, 70; in historiography, 83,
    91–4; and History Circle, 38; and Interna-
    tional Boundary Commission, 41, 49–50;

and lake village, 41, 50; life cycle, 50; and memory, 94; name of Sumas warrior *Qwál*, 61; and oral tradition, 86; in politics of drainage, 60–73; as "punctuation," 49; at Sumas Lake, 21, 70; Sumas Lake as retreat from, 21; *t'ehm-eh-KWIY-ehl* as retreat from, 60

Mosquito Story, 86

Mumford, Lewis, 11

Museum of Vertebrate Zoology, Berkeley, 48, 107n90

Myvatan, Lake, 46

narrative: oral, 13, 81; written, 13, 81, 88. *See also* oral tradition; Origin Story; Progress Story

Nash, Roderick, 31

National Research Council, 69

Ned, Chief (Selesmlton), 32, 33

Nelson, Theodor, 8

New Western History, 7, 98n18

New Westminster, 51

Nile valley, 93

Nooksack, 46, 50, 87, 103n10

North Sea, 48

Northwest Game Act, 67

nostalgia, 14

Oliver, Premier John, 67

O'Meara, Arthur, 36

opening: definition of, 3, 7

oral history: and anthropology, 18; in archives, 21; and historiography, 20–1; ideology of, 26; listening to, 20; as place of mediation, 40; as process, 18; and public history, 26; and surprise, 94; as technique for gathering power, 16

oral tradition, 78, 81, 85, 88

Orchard, Imbert, 19, 23, 85, 87, 88

Origin Story, 86, 87, 89

Ormsby, Margaret, 7, 83

ospreys, 50

owl, great gray, 57

Parr, Joy, 38

Paull, Andrew, 34, 36, 38

picnicking, 22, 23, 28, 35, 38

place, 10, 100n1; interactions with story, 88–91

population, 51, 53; repopulation, 87

Postman, Neil, 11

potato, sweet, *xwoqw'o:ls*, 50, 74

Power, Charlie, 26

Pre-emption Act of 1860, 51

Progress Story, 82–4, 89

Railway Belt, 43, 57

reserves, 51–7, 66; Chilliwack, 36, 55; and Indian Act, 98n13; Matsqui, 55; and Sumas Dyking Act, 55; Sumas no. 2, 53; Sumas no. 5 (Aylechootlook), 72; Sumas no. 6 (Kilgard), 16, 23, 31, 66, 78, 85, 87; Sumas no. 7, 16, 31, 66; Upper Sumas and Lower Sumas, 51. *See also* McKenna-McBride Commission

residential schools, 23, 81, 88

Rheingold, Howard, 14

romanticizing, 14, 23, 38–9, 44
Rosaldo, Renato, 18
rose, wild, 23
roundfish, 44

salmon, 23, 63, 69, 74, 88; Humpy, 86
Sam, Louis, 57
sandpiper, 63
Scott, Duncan Campbell, 61
sedgebirds, 51
Simmons, I.G., 16, 48
Sinclair, Frank, 72
skating, 25, 38
Slotkin, Richard, 9
smallpox, 53
Smith, Allan, 7
Smith, Sam, 68
Snyder, Gary, 24
spawning, 33, 63, 69. See also salmon
Special Committee hearing on claims of Allied Indian Tribes, 36
Sproat, Gilbert Malcolm, 53–5, 57
Stó:lō: meaning of, 3; See also McKenna-McBride Commission; oral history; oral tradition; population; reserves; Sumas; time
story: interactions with place, 88–91
sturgeon, 23, 50, 63, 65, 74, 88
Sumas: as ecosystem, 9; as Internet node, 13; lake bottom, 4, 5, 75–9, 86–8; lake size (1894), 16, 47; meaning of, 5, 97n2; and pleasure, 18, 24, 40; as resource base, 21–6, 33–4, 48–51, 74; as wasteland, 14, 16. See

also mosquitoes; Origin Story; Progress Story; reserves; Sumas Camp; Sumas Lake drainage; Sumas South
Sumas Camp, 49
Sumas Dyking Act, 54–5, 57
Sumas Lake drainage, 5, 16, 18, 60–74; and archives, 43–4; and Chief Ned, 33; early plans and legislation for, 29, 54–7, 59; protest against, 33, 55; technology, 6, 48, 74. See also Sumas
Sumas River, 49, 50
Sumas South, 87
swallows, 51
swans, 49, 51, 63, 67
swimming, 6, 18, 23

Tennant, Paul, 53
Thompson, Paul, 26
time, 12–13, 86; and temporal frameworks, 36, 89
Treaty for International Protection of Migratory Birds, 66
trout, 23, 63, 70
Trutch, Joseph, 27, 50, 53
Tufte, Edward, 10

Under an Open Sky, 8
Union of B.C. Indian Chiefs, 29
Uslick, Mrs Harry, 87, 89

Vankoughnet, Lawrence, 56–7
Vedder Canal, 12
Vedder River, 46, 72, 83

Vienneau, Janelle, 21, 24
Vowell, Superintendent, 63

Walkem, George, 55
Walker, Katie, 20
water rights, 36
Watts, George, 38, 39
Wells, Casey, 82
Wells, Oliver, 21, 85, 108n113
wetlands, 43, 48. *See* Sumas
Whatcom County, 9, 46
White, George, 83, 85, 89
White, Hayden, 12, 13

Whitehead, A.N., 11
Wilson, Charles, 49, 50
Women's Institute, 31
Worster, Donald, 84

Xwelitem, 98n13. *See also* colonialism

Yarrow, 84, 87
York, Jim, 21, 31
York, Nora, 25
York, Mrs Thomas Fraser, 21, 31

Zink, Fred, 24